How To Hear
God's Voice

By Arthur Bailey

How To Hear
God's Voice

By Arthur Bailey
Arthur Bailey Ministries
PO Box 49744
Charlotte, NC 28277

Published and produced in the United States of America
ISBN: 978-15086508-2-9
Library of Congress Control Number: 2015903438
Edited by Higher Heart Productions

For more information visit www.ArthurBaileyMinistries.com

Text is 12 point Calibri and Times New Roman

This booklet is designed to accompany the Arthur Bailey Ministries DVD teaching of the same title.

Part 1 Message:

Today we're going to be talking about **How to Hear God's Voice**; or how to hear the voice of YeHoVaH. I wanted to share this teaching with you. As I've tried to figure out how I am going to help you learn how to hear the voice of YeHoVaH, the only way that I can do that is to share some scripture with you and to share some experience. What I have found is that from an experience point of view, many of us experience a lot of the same things.

The enemy tries to convince us that we might be the only one experiencing something; especially if it's bad. If we're having a problem in our marriage, if we're having a problem with our children, if we're having a problem with our parents — you know, the enemy tries to convince us that we're the only one on the face of the planet who is having that problem. How many — if you're married, let me see your hand.

Now if you're married, have you ever had marital problems? Let me see your hand. Imagine if you've had marital problems. The world has what they call these focus groups. They have homogeneous groups. You know, if you're an alcoholic or a former alcoholic you can go to A.A. (Alcoholics Anonymous). In A.A. you can share your story.

> "Hi, I'm Arthur, and I am, you know, a former alcoholic."

And they say:

> "What? You're still an alcoholic."

No, I'm no longer one. You see, that's why I stopped going to A.A. When I got delivered from alcohol; from alcoholism, I was no longer an alcoholic. Now I know for those of you who are still in A.A. that might be cutting against the grain. But this is not an A.A. meeting. Anyway, as we go to these groups, you know people go to counseling sessions and group therapy. In these group therapies, what people find is that,

> "Hey, you know your situation is very similar to mine. You're having some of the same problems. Are you telling me your son, your daughter, your husband, your wife...?"

> "Yes, Yes, Yes, Yes."

People are shocked to find that they are having some of the same problems other people are having or that other people are having some of the same issues that they're having. How many of you know this is the same with the word? You see, people want to start off, and again on *Facebook* people want to say,

> "You don't need any man to teach you."

You know, that's in the Bible. But how many of you know that those who wrote these things would encourage people to:

> "Follow me as I follow Messiah"?

Many of us learn what we know not from what people told us, but from what we have watched, seen and experienced. Compare that with what we've been told. Many of us learn how to be a man from watching men. If we didn't have a good man in our home, then we don't know how to be a good man. You know many of you, you watch. What does it mean to be a woman; a Godly woman?

The Bible says for Godly women, aged women to teach the younger woman how to love their husbands. Why do they need to be taught? There are some instructions. Aged men are to train up younger men. You are to instruct them.

Don't rebuke an elder. I mean there are certain instructions. What's going to happen is that the experience that we have in life is designed not just for us, but for those who are coming behind us.

One of the problems here in the United States of America is that we have a tendency to discard our elders. When people get to a certain age, we put them away. We don't want to hear them.

The age is now getting younger and younger. By the age of twelve or thirteen we start thinking our parents are idiots — that they don't know anything; that they don't know that times are different. Everything has changed, and what they've experienced — that's not the way it's done today. Children younger and younger and younger are discarding the wisdom of the elders. It's a culture. We've got people who are going to the graves who've got all of this experience. They would sit down and talk to you about things if you sat down and talked to them about them. But people think,

> "Well you know, you've got the same Holy
> Spirit that I have so I don't need you. I can
> follow God all by myself."

That is partly true. But how many of you know there are some traps along the way? There are some detours along the way. There are some rabbit trails along the way. There is some enticing along the way. There are other voices along the way, and sometimes these other voices sound like it might be Him. We've got to distinguish His voice from the other voices, and that's what this teaching is about today.

From *Genesis* to *Revelation* we see that YeHoVaH is speaking. He opens the first few verses with:

> "Then God Said — Then Elohim said."

YeHoVaH comes onto the scene talking. In *Revelation* the Bible closes with the Spirit and the bride saying what?

"Come."

There is communication by YeHoVaH from the beginning of the book to the very end of the book and everywhere in between.

Throughout biblical history, believers and non-believers alike have heard the voice of God, and we are going to look at that. We see experience from the scripture along with our own personal experience. The experience of those who have gone before us will help us to navigate the troubled path that is laid before us — full of pitfalls.

In the world they have what they call mentors, coaches; people whom folks pay good money to show them how to do business. Anybody ever heard of mentors or life coaches? Well, you know we are life coaches, and we are real life coaches because the word of life, we have.

Adam and Eve along with their murdering son Cain all heard the creator's voice. Prophets, Kings, Pharaohs, and even the common working man had encounters and were given direction directly from YeHoVaH's mouth. Here's what Moses said. Moses said as he was speaking to the children of Israel:

> "YeHoVaH humbled you, causing you to hunger; and then feeding you with manna, which neither you nor your fathers had known; to teach you that man does not live on bread alone, but on every word that comes from the mouth of YeHoVaH."

Our life is dependent upon the word that comes from His mouth. Yeshua said:

> "It is written."

Now he is quoting Moses here.

> "Man does not live on bread alone, but on every word that comes from the mouth of God."

Now here he is talking to the devil in this vision; in this passage, where the devil is saying,

> "If you be the Son of God, turn these stones into bread."

He responds by quoting the Torah. He said in another place,

> "But he that enters in by the door is the shepherd of the sheep. To him the porter opens and the sheep hear his voice. And he calls his own sheep by name and leads them out. And when he puts forth his own sheep, he goes before them and the sheep follow him for they know his voice. A stranger they will not follow, but will flee from him for they know not the voice of the strangers."

What he is saying here folks is that there are voices, and then there is the voice. There are the voices, and then there is the voice.

Some of you may have heard this story. I remember as a young man, we lived next to a park. It is interesting that practically all of the places we've lived since I've been an adult, have been close to a park. We've always been in some proximity. As a matter of fact, the house that we lived in the longest; you walk out of our backyard to the fence and you are right there in the park.

It's something that growing up next to a park as a child put something in me where most of the places — you know I didn't think okay, we're going to buy a house and it's going to be next to the park. It just happened to work out that way.

What is that saying? There are things that are deposited in us — things that we have experienced as children, that simply play out in our lives. This is why in some cases we literally have to come to a place where we have to put up a stop. That is because if you just live your life; if you are left up to yourself, what you'll do is you have already been placed on a path by those who have gone before you, whether they were good or evil. You will find yourself following the footsteps of the path that has already been laid before you. I was following in the footsteps of my Dad and didn't even know it.

The very things that I had hated, I had become. Anybody know what I'm talking about? My Dad taught me some good things, but he also taught me some bad things. When he taught me bad things, he didn't say,

> "Arthur, sit down, I want to teach you some
> bad stuff."

No. He taught me bad things by example. I'm following example. I'm following a pattern. I'm following what I'm being raised in. This is what David was talking about when he said,

> "Listen, I was born in sin and raised in
> iniquity. I was surrounded by lawless
> people."

We become like our environment. It's just automatic. So we have to at some point, STOP. I had to come to a place where I had to denounce my Dad, my blood line and my family. It was only then that I could properly relate to my Dad. As long as I was under that "anointing" (if you would), that spirit, I was subjected.

As children, our parents are always our parents. If they've drilled in us that you honor your mom, you honor your dad and you listen, what that meant (at least the way I interpret it) is that honoring my parents was doing what my parents said to do. Did anybody else interpret it that way? We get to a point where we say okay, at what point do I stop doing what my parents say do, and it is not being dishonoring?

When you begin to walk with the Almighty, the Almighty is going to say some things to you just like He said to Abraham,

> "Abraham, it's time for you to leave your folks' house."

As long as we are with our folks, our parents, our older brothers, our older sisters — I was raised up in an environment where you do what your sisters tell you. My sisters were my surrogate mothers. My brothers were my surrogate fathers. I had to listen to my older brothers. I couldn't say,

> "I'm not going to listen to you. Who made you the boss of me?"

That's a smack down! It's a smack down on the spot. And as soon as my parents get home they said,

> "Do you know what your boy said to me?"

That's another smack down because I'd been given direct instructions that:

> "When I'm not here, you listen to them."

You see, somewhere that got twisted, because younger children today for some reason don't think they have to listen to their older brothers and sisters, and that's unfortunate.

When you get to a point where you begin to follow the voice of the Almighty, it's going to bring you to a place where it is time to leave your parents' house. It's time to leave your brothers and sisters. Let me tell you something. Whether you realize it or not, your older brothers and sisters and your parents still have power over you.

When you come into the environment that they are in, for some reason, automatically you simply acquiesce back to child-likeness. Anybody ever have that issue? You know, you get around your brothers and sisters. You get around your parents. My wife used to tease me. Here I am this, you know, I'm the man of my house. I'm the head of my home, and I get around Mama and it's like,

> "Yes Ma'am. Yes Ma'am. Yes Ma'am. Yes
> Ma'am. No Ma'am. Yes Ma'am."

That was it. That's what we were taught. "Yes Ma'am" and "No Ma'am." "Yes Sir" and "No Sir." I remember the first time I said:

> "Yeah."

It didn't go over well.

> "Uh huh."

That didn't go over well either, but he says here that Yeshua continued to say:

> "And a stranger they will not follow"

This indicates that there are lots of voices out there, folks. And the question is, whose voice are you listening to? Have you ever heard the voice of God? It's a question. Do you know what His voice sounds like? Whose voice are you following?

Interchangeably these kinds of things happen. Last week as we were here, at the end of service, I called out someone who had back pain, and then they had pain going down their leg. Anybody remember me calling that out? Nobody responded, nobody, and then online it's like, nobody responded. Well, I got home and I had received a phone call from someone who was online, who called their Mom, and said:

> "Mom, I think he was praying — he was talking about you."

So the Mother called me, and I called the Mother back because she left a message. She said,

> "My daughter told me you had prayed."

She asked me what time it was, and it was around two o'clock that day. She said,

> "Last week at two o'clock that day I was crying out to God. The pain in my back was so excruciating."

Prior to getting that phone call, I'm standing here feeling like I've missed it. I mean I've missed it. I knew just as surely as the voice — I knew that voice. I knew as surely as I was standing here that He had called this out. Okay?

So we go, and I pray to heal. I thought you know, this lady wasn't even on the chat. She wasn't there. The daughter was on chat, but the Mother who needed the prayer wasn't on chat. I'm thinking in my mind, this person that I'm talking to — for me to call it out, they should have heard me.

I found some resolve in the fact that okay, maybe this is one of those proxy situations. Anybody ever prayed by proxy? You know, you stand in the gap for someone else? Well lo and behold I went to bed, woke up the next day, and then I got this phone call from Ed down in Atlanta, who was online. And Ed said,

> "I wanted to just call you and let you know
> that when you called that out, it was me.
> And when you prayed, the pain in my back
> went down my leg and out of my body."

Now I'm really feeling justified in the fact. Now what about the Mother? She entered into the prayer. What am I trying to say? There is a time. Like do you remember when Yeshua was at Solomon's colonnade and there was this man who had been laying there for some time? He looked at him and said,

> "Do you want to be healed?"

And the man said,

> "Well, I have nobody to place me into the
> pool when the water is troubled."

He was waiting for someone to place him in the pool when the water was troubled. Somebody got in ahead of him, you see. There is a time when the presence of the Almighty is there, and when it is, you can enter into it.

When someone is ministering prophetically like that, you may say,

> "Well, that might be me"

Or whatever the case may be, it doesn't matter. When prayer is going forward as I shared; when I do the Aaronic benediction, that is an opportunity for you to enter into the prayer and the power of the Almighty.

So Ed shared with me. He says,

> "Yeah, that was me."

Now I'm feeling a little bit better. I'm glad that Mother got her healing. But at the same time, I'm questioning whether or not my hearing is getting dull. I'm sharing this with you because there are going to be times where you are going to question whether or not you are hearing. But here's what I've learned. If I sense it's the Father leading, I'm going to step out. I'm going to call it even though no one responds.

It took me back to several years ago when we were running a storefront non-profit. These two ladies came into our facility. They were looking for services that we provided. While they were sitting there, the Father showed me that there was some lesbian activity going on. It was not because of what they were doing, because they weren't touching each other. I said to the one lady,

> "You know, the Father has given me a word.
> Do you mind if I share it with you?"

I shared this word with her and the woman said to me,

> "Preacher, you are so far off, it's pathetic."

That's what she said to me.

> "You are off!"

And her friend sitting next to her said,

> "Why are you lying to the preacher? That
> man just told you about yourself."

And she said,

> "Um Reverend, please forgive her. She's a
> lesbian, and I'm her mate."

Now the point is, that when she said,

> "Preacher you are so far off,"

It's like somebody took a dagger if you would, and just pierced my heart. That is because here I am standing out on what I believe the Father is saying and the response was one of negativity. The Father would not allow that to stand.

He prompted that young lady sitting next to her to rise up and confirm every word that I had just spoken.

There are times ladies and gentlemen, when you hear the voice of the Almighty and you step out on it, that you may seem like you're way out there on a limb. This is what causes people to hesitate — to not act. I would much rather step out on hearing His voice and miss it and be wrong, than to think I hear His voice and not move on it. That word may be the very word that saves that person's life. And here it is, now because the Father prompted me to speak and I didn't speak, their blood is on my hands.

I was looking at the news yesterday. I don't know if you all know about this situation where there were firefighters who were called to a fire. When they got there, they were ambushed. Well, they came to find out that the guy who ambushed them had felonies and wasn't allowed to purchase a gun. It turns out that the neighbor of this guy, a young lady, bought the guns for this fellow, and now she is in jail. She was an accessory to murder.

Why am I bringing that up? I'm bringing that up because there are times when you participate in something — I'm sure that when she bought those guns, she didn't think that one day this move that I'm making right now could possibly land me ten years in prison and a $250,000 fine.

But guess what? The guy who ambushed the fire department left a suicide note. In the suicide note he said that he got the guns from her. Now we sit here and we think about this. But think about how many times we have been the accessory to someone's lawless deeds — how we've covered up for someone who we knew was doing wrong and we lied.

The thing about it is that we may not ever have to face the court of human opinion from judges who sit on benches, but we're going to have to face the ultimate judge. We are not to be partakers in other peoples' sin. That's the flip side of the Father telling you to do something and then you don't do it. I would much rather hear His voice or believe I'm hearing His voice; step out and miss it, than to hear His voice and not be sure and not do anything.

While at the same time, evil communications corrupt good character. I say you need to stop being with, and hanging out with people who aren't interested in hearing His voice. Whose voice are you following?

In this teaching we're going to find out some important information that I believe is going to help you identify and distinguish. Those of you who are young, you young people; this is especially important for you because you can learn now and not make some of the mistakes that some of us older people have made.

I am so fortunate that Father has given me opportunities to redeem some things that I have done. He's redeemed my family on my behalf. Now I feel that He is redeeming a lot of other things in our lives; because the Father IS a redeemer.

When we turn our hearts toward Him, the things that we think that we've lost – the people that may turn on us because we are walking in His way, Father has a way of redeeming all of that; even the pain of walking away from family members who aren't interested in hearing the truth, or the abuse that you get from brothers and sisters and aunts and uncles because you try to share the truth with them and they reject it.

The people who turn on you; the friends who don't want anything to do with you because they think you are weird – you're always talking that "God stuff." And do you know that Father has a way if you don't faint, of redeeming all of that. Those people who turned on you, those people who said things about you; those family members who didn't invite you to the Christmas party and who didn't invite you to the birthday, they didn't invite you to that stuff because you don't celebrate that stuff anymore. Father has a way of redeeming it — of redeeming you and it's when you least likely know.

You know, I received an email from a minister that I ordained; asking me some questions. Those of you who were here on Thursday night, you heard that story. This weekend I received a call from my nephew. I haven't talked to this young man since he was little and he called me up. He called me up because he found our phone number on our web site. I'm finding that our web site is reaching all kinds of people, even my own family members, you see.

From the beginning of creation, YeHoVaH has been communicating with man.

> **Gen 2:6** "YeHoVaH commanded the man, saying, 'of every tree of the garden you may freely eat: but of the tree of the knowledge of good and evil, you shall not eat of it: for in the day you eat thereof, you shall surely die.'"

Here we see Father having communication with Adam.

> **Gen 3:1** "Now the serpent was more subtle than any beast of the field which YeHoVaH God had made. And he said unto the woman, 'Yea, hath God said, ye shall not eat of every tree of the garden?'"

Automatically now, we've got the voice of the Father communicating. There is another voice in the garden.

> **Gen 3:2** "And the woman said unto the serpent, 'we may eat of the fruit of the trees of the garden:'"

As you can see there, here's the first he said/she said conversation.

"Well he said,"

But then it's "she said." We see the enemy speaking to the woman after the Father has spoken.

Listening to the wrong voice will lead to wrong doing. Wrong doing will always lead to hiding unless you are just flat-out LAWLESS. Some people are just flat-out lawless, so they don't hide anymore. Some people are still hiding. Listening to the wrong voice will lead to a life of curses and death as *Deuteronomy* 28:15 says:

> "But it shall come to pass, if you will not hearken unto the voice of YeHoVaH your Elohim, to observe, to do all his commandments and his statutes which I command you this day; that all these curses will come upon you, and overtake you."

This is the word of YeHoVaH to the children of Israel. Moses is communicating as he is about to go. He is about to leave. You know, this is the last of Moses' life, and he's just recapping what Father has said. Listening to the voice of YeHoVaH will lead to a life of prominence and blessings. This is what he says in *Deuteronomy* 28:1. He says:

> "And it shall come to pass, if you hearken diligently unto the voice of YeHoVaH thy Elohim, to observe and to do all his commands which I command you this day, that YeHoVaH your God will set you high above all nations of the earth."

He is going to raise you prominently in the sight of all those people who cursed you, who told you that you were under a curse, who told you that you are going back under the Law, who told you that you are fallen from grace.

> "And all these blessings will come on you
> and overtake you. If you hearken unto the
> voice of YeHoVaH your Elohim."

Prominence and blessings come from obeying the voice.

> "And they heard the voice of YeHoVaH."

Now back to the garden.

> "They heard the voice of YeHoVaH walking
> in the garden in the cool of the day and
> Adam and Eve, Adam and his wife rather,
> hid themselves from the presence of
> YeHoVaH amongst the trees of the garden."

Now notice here in most versions of the Bible, it doesn't have Adam and Eve. Anybody got a Bible you are reading? Could you tell me, what does it say there? Now I'm about to make a point. It's important that you catch what I am about to say in the next few slides. I need you to see in *Genesis* chapter three verse eight. What does it read and who's got it?

Adam and his wife; they hid. Okay, anybody else? The man and his wife. Anybody else? Something different? So what we are seeing here — say what? Wife — the man and his wife.

> "And YeHoVaH God called unto Adam, and
> said unto him, 'Where are you?' And he
> said, 'I heard your voice in the garden, and I
> was afraid, because I was naked; and I hid
> myself.'"

Listening to the wrong voice will lead to fear. This is why you can't be listening to these voices out there that are telling you,

> "You know, you need to run to the hills."

The Bible didn't say run to the hills from which cometh your help. He said LOOK to the hills from which cometh your help. Your help is coming OUT from the hills, not causing you to run to the hills and hide.

Listening to the wrong voice will cause you to feel exposed, uncovered; naked. Listening to the wrong voice will bring guilt. It will bring shame and ultimately it will lead to hiding. When we do what is opposed to the word, we don't want to be around people in the word.

A young lady said something to me. Now she and her husband are pastoring a congregation in Tennessee. I noticed that when I was in this particular church as an Elder, that every time I would minister, she would leave. And so one day I asked her,

> "You know, why do you always leave when I'm preaching? Everybody else can stand up there and preach and you sit there, but when I get up and preach, you leave."

And she said,

> "I always feel like you're looking right through me."

I can't tell you how many times I have had people say stuff like that to me. I remember a mother brought her son. She was so excited about the service. She brought her son, and that day the gifting; the anointing of prophecy was upon me. I began to prophesy to that young man. It freaked him out. He told his mother,

> "I am never coming back to that church again because you've told that preacher about me. You've told the preacher everything about me."

19

She had never said a word. I have had that happen to me on numerous occasions. It's not that I'm seeing what a person is in, it is that the Father gives me words and I speak those words. I would love to say that every time I have spoken that it has been His voice. That's not the case.

Gen 3:11   "and he said, 'who told you?'"

Now you need to pay specific attention. Adam said,

"I hid because I was naked."

YeHoVaH says,

"Who told you, you were naked?"

Now that's a very simple phrase, so something happened. You see, one of the things that I think the Father did is that He gave us His instructions. What the deceiver does is that he comes alongside us and starts — you know the Bible says he's the accuser. He's the accuser of the brethren. He doesn't just accuse the brethren, he accuses God to men.

"Did God say that you can't — I mean did He really mean that? Did He literally say that? What does that mean in the Greek?"

I mean this is the conversation and the whole idea is to cast doubt. Because the moment somebody says,

"Well, what does that mean in the Hebrew?"

What they are saying is that I know what that means in the Hebrew, but you are too stupid to know what it says in the Hebrew. And when you say:

"I don't know what it means in the Hebrew."

They're going to tell you what that literally means in the Hebrew and the moment they go there, they've automatically set themself up higher above you to look smarter and wiser. Now you feel diminished and dumb. These are some of the tricks. You may hear a pastor say,

> "Well listen. I've been to seminary, have you?"

Okay, you've been to seminary. What does that have to do with the conversation? I know better. I know more. I know more than you! This is what they are getting to. You are too dumb. You didn't go to train.

> "I've been trained."

You see, the whole idea is to cause you to doubt your ability to hear from the Father yourself. After a while you become convinced (if you are not careful), that:

> "Other people can hear His voice better than I can, so I'm not gonna trust the things that I hear. I'm going to trust what they hear. So you go and talk to God and tell me what He says and I will do it."

Did you hear that before?

> "Who told you that you were naked?"

Adam was naked all along. There are some things that are so obvious, they are not even obvious. He's there all along and all of a sudden after he has done what he's done, the devil says,

> "Oh, by the way, did you know you didn't have any clothes on?"

> "I don't?"

> "No!"

And he's laughing at him. Now he's feeling even more diminished because he knows that he has done wrong. So now it's,

> "Oh my God, what have I done?"

The Father calls him, and He does what? He says:

> "Have you eaten of the tree whereof I commanded you that you should not eat?"

The Father knew that in the disobedience of the command, it was going to give him knowledge that all he had to do was to go to the Father and ask. But do you know what? Sometimes people raise questions and suspicion in areas that — you don't even think about stuff like that. I mean all of a sudden now they've put something in your head that you didn't think on your own. They've sowed doubt. They've sowed some confusion. Always be aware of people who will speak evil about someone else.

There are six things the Father hates. The seventh is an abomination — he that sows discord among the brethren. Whenever people bring information that is going to cause discord between you and somebody else, you need to know that is not from the Father; because the Father hates it. Now notice what he says:

> "And the man said, 'the woman, the woman.'"

Why did he call her the woman? Because that's what he named her. Now wait a minute, didn't he name her Eve? No, he *renamed* her.

> "The man said, 'the woman whom you gave to me to be with me, she gave me of the tree, and I did eat.'"

Listening to the wrong voice will lead to the blame game. It will cause you not to take responsibility for your actions. Now someone else may rightfully be guilty for what they did, but your action — you are responsible for. Nobody can make you do anything. They can give you wrong information. They can give you bad information. They can give you information period and you can respond to it.

You are responsible for your response to whatever information people bring to you or whatever situation you are confronted with. You are responsible for your action. The moment you do not take responsibility for your action is the moment you do exactly what Adam is doing here — blaming somebody else.

The majority of the people grow up blaming other people for their mishaps; for the state and the condition that their life is in.

> "And YeHoVaH said unto the woman, 'What is this that you have done?' And the woman said, 'The serpent beguiled me, and I did eat.' And YeHoVaH said unto the serpent, 'Because you have done this, you are cursed above all cattle, and above every beast of the field; upon your belly shall you go, and dust shall you eat all the days of your life.'"

Now I want to share with you a nugget here. Maybe you have thought about this, and maybe you haven't. At no point in scripture had YeHoVaH spoken to the serpent prior to this point. He didn't say to the serpent,

> "Now listen. I want you to stay out of the garden, and don't you dare beguile the woman."

He did say to Adam and to the woman,

> "Don't you eat from the tree."

Do you see this? The man and the woman by their own actions brought a curse upon the serpent. He was just having a conversation in the garden, so why was the serpent cursed?

Adam and Eve had been given instructions; not the serpent. They had been given instructions over everything. YeHoVaH had given them dominion over everything except each other. It was Adam who called the serpent the serpent. They were responsible for the serpent. The very thing that they were responsible for — because they failed to listen to the voice of YeHoVaH, that caused them not only to have to pay for their actions, but they now had to pay for the action of the serpent.

Wait a minute. Wasn't the serpent the devil? That's what he is referred to in the book of *Revelation*, but that is neither here nor there. We've got a serpent in the garden — a serpent who obviously had been in the garden for some time because hey, the woman is having a conversation with him. She is not afraid of the serpent.

When you cause someone to stumble, you will not be held guiltless. You see the serpent caused a stumbling block, but the woman didn't have to listen.

> "Adam where are you?"

> "Well the woman you gave me — well the serpent."

In *Mathew* 18:6, Yeshua says:

> "But whosoever shall offend one of these little ones which believe in me, it were better for him that a millstone were hanged about his neck, and that he were drowned in the depth of the sea."

The word here; the word that is in the King James, says:

"If whosoever shall offend."

"Offend" here is the Greek word *skan-dal-id'-zo;* which means to entrap, to trip up; to cause to stumble.

You see, information that you give that is not accurate (especially when you pass on rumors), could create a stumbling block for other people — information, religion, theology, traditions. You know?

Somebody who wants to genuinely know what the word of YeHoVaH says concerning Hanukkah asks someone who has been taught that Hanukkah is about a nine branch menorah. You're passing on information that is not true. Then someone comes along and dispels the nine branch menorah.

Someone who has adopted the Hanukkah celebration of lighting a nine branch menorah just came out of the church and the traditions. Now it is exposed that they are operating in tradition. How do you think that person who has left tradition only to enter into tradition by somebody else's communication is responding to the tradition that they have been given by well-meaning Messianics?

This person now wants to throw away the Hanukkah tree, the Hanukkah menorah and Yeshua. That is because just as Santa Claus has been exposed in Christianity and Sunday worship exposed in Christianity, now Hanukkah Harry, the Hanukkah bush and the menorah for Hanukkah are exposed in the Messianic faith.

I have jumped out of one tradition into another tradition. Who am I to believe? This is why you can't be sharing leaven. This is why you can't be communicating doctrine. You can't be communicating tradition because someone is going to come along, expose the tradition and now the person who thought that they were on solid ground is tripped up again because of you. He said,

"Well, what's wrong with it?"

It is not Bible.

> **Psa 1:1** "Blessed is the man that walks not in the counsel of the ungodly, nor stands in the way of sinners, nor sits in the seat of the scornful. But his delight is in the law of YeHoVaH; and in his law does he meditate day and night."

> **Psa 1:3** "And he shall be like a tree planted by the rivers of water, that brings forth his fruit in his season; his leaf also shall not wither; and whatsoever he does shall prosper."

Who is this man — the man who walks not in the counsel of the ungodly? Now understand something. Eve walked in the counsel of the serpent. Adam walked in the counsel of Eve — all created perfect. Was Eve ungodly? Was she fallen when she told Adam to eat from the tree?

You've got the creation of YeHoVaH giving counsel to her husband and that ultimately causes all of them to come under the judgment of the Almighty. Sometimes Godly people can give ungodly counsel. The woman received ungodly counsel from the serpent and passed it onto her husband.

> **Gen 3:17** "And unto Adam he said, 'because you hast hearkened unto the voice of thy wife'"

There's another voice. We've got the voice of YeHoVaH. We've got the voice of the serpent. We've got the voice of the wife. But notice what He said.

> "Because you've harkened to the voice of your wife"

Not to the voice of Eve.

"And has eaten of the tree of which I commanded thee, saying, 'you shall not eat of it:' cursed is the ground for your sake; in sorrow shall you eat of it all the days of your life;"

Gen 3:20 "And Adam called his wife's name Eve; because she was the mother of all living."

You see, Adam who had named all the animals and his wife, now renames his wife. This is a separation folks. The one now becomes two again. You see, the two were supposed to be one. But what Adam does, is he separates. Get this. YeHoVaH named the man and the woman Adam. Bible.

Gen 5:1 "This is the book of the generations of Adam. In the day that Elohim created man, in the likeness of Elohim made he him; male and female created he them; and blessed them, and YeHoVaH called their name Adam, in the day when they were created."

YeHoVaH called her Adam. Adam first named her woman. This is what happened.

Gen 2:23 "And Adam said, 'This is now bone of my bones, and flesh of my flesh: she shall be called Woman.'"

He gives her a name, and what does he call her? Woman. What did YeHoVaH call her? Adam.

Gen 2:24   "Therefore shall a man leave his father and his mother, and shall cleave unto his wife: and they shall be one flesh"

Man and woman are named Adam — a lesson from Eve.

Gen 4:1   "And Adam knew Eve his wife; and she conceived, and bare Cain, and said, 'I have gotten a man from YeHoVaH.'"

Now you've got to understand something. Although YeHoVaH had pronounced punishment upon Eve; banned them from the garden and made them work, Eve still recognized YeHoVaH as the source of her blessings — Eve the woman, Eve formerly call the woman, formerly called Adam. You see in the book of *Genesis*, Eve is named Adam, Woman and Eve. The last two names, the man gave her. I just want you to ponder on that for awhile because Adam called her those names. You say,

"Well why are you pushing that? Why are you making that such an issue?"

It is because the Father didn't see any difference. Even though sin had entered into the world and infected mankind, YeHoVaH still communicated with fallen man.

Gen 4:3   "And in the process of time it came to pass, that Cain brought of the fruit of the ground an offering unto YeHoVaH."

Gen 4:4   "And Abel, he also brought of the firstlings of his flock and of the fat thereof. And YeHoVaH had respect unto Abel and to his offering:"

Gen 4:5   "But unto Cain and to his offering he had not respect. And Cain was very wroth, and his countenance fell."

He was angry. That is no different than today. You know, I'm watching. Do you know that children compete for their parents' attention?

"Mama look at me."

"No, Mama look at me."

"Mama look at me, I can do that too, I can do it even better."

Children are always competing it seems, for the parents' attention. The Father — and I wonder how did Cain know that the Father didn't like his offering? I dare say that the Father told him, because after all, they are in communication. Now in my Baptist Church when they said that, you know this is just ridiculous when I think about it.

Let me tell you something about denominations, folks. Denominations lead us through the Bible. A denomination does not encourage Bible reading. It encourages memorizing scripture. Here is a typical service:

"Okay, take your Bibles and turn with me."

"Okay, take your Bibles and turn with me to."

You can be in church for twenty years being told where to turn, you see. I was taught in my Baptist Church that when Adam and Eve fell, God stopped communicating with men. That's what they told me. Anybody else ever heard that? You know, that's what they said.

Now I'm seeing that YeHoVaH is talking to Cain. Wait a minute. Cain just murdered his brother. Adam and Eve have been kicked out of the garden.

I would also suggest to you and I think there might be some truth to this, that it's very possible based on the judgment that YeHoVaH pronounced on Eve — think about it. Your pain in childbirth will greatly increase. How would she know? How would she know? How would she be able to tell the difference between no pain and increased pain? Is it possible that Cain and Abel may have been born before? How would she know the difference?

Just a thought. I mean I think about stuff like that. It's like, you are going to tell me something but I don't know any difference. Hey, my first child is like this, so that's the way having children is. But is it possible that maybe she could tell the difference based upon the fact from experience? We see that they are having this conversation. YeHoVaH now says,

> "Cain, why are you angry? And why is your face fallen? Why is your countenance fallen?"

> **Gen 4:7**   "If you do well, shall you not be accepted?"

Now we see YeHoVaH communicating with Cain. But what is not here is Cain talking to YeHoVaH. Yet Cain knows something is wrong.

> "And if you do not do well, sin lies at the door and unto you shall be his desire, and you must rule over it."

Folks, this is one of the most powerful verses in all of scripture because this is still applicable to us today. You must rule over it. That's what we rule over. We don't rule over one another. Now I can give you some — that's another sermon. Just as YeHoVaH instructed Cain, we too must rule over our evil desires or our evil desires will rule over us. You know, Jeremiah says that the heart is deceitful above all things. Who can know it?

I said this before and some folks got upset with me. The reason why I try to be transparent is because I know me. I know my thoughts. You see, I have thoughts. You all have thoughts. If people knew you thought like that, you would be ashamed to share. I'm not afraid to tell you I have thoughts. I think thoughts that I know are not right. And if I acted on some I see — I used to act on some of those thoughts and it got me in a lot of trouble.

There is a way that seems right to man, but the end thereof is destruction. For some reason we think that hey, everybody else may get caught, but I am too slick. I'm not going to get caught. Well, that doesn't apply to me. I'm smarter than that.

I would love sometime — I don't think I would do this, but I could imagine sometimes if there was a device that you put onto somebody — an invisible device that you could put onto your husband or your wife while they are asleep. And when they get up they don't know it is on. The invisible device is tied to a monitor and it visually monitors the thoughts that they are having.

Can you imagine if somebody put that on you; when you are thinking about cheating, lying, stealing, or murdering? Or how about when nobody is around and you are daydreaming? What about when you are fantasizing? I know people want to play all holier than thou, but I know me and I know that there is nothing good.

> "Well, wait a minute, aren't you redeemed?
> Aren't you born again?"

Yes, my spirit man has been regenerated, but I still live in this flesh. My mind needs to be renewed. I have to renew my mind. My mind did not become renewed when I became born again. Neither did yours. The things that we think about saying but don't say; the things that we think about doing, but don't do — and yet we can sit around and sit in judgment with others; concerning others.

If only the monitor was hooked up to your thoughts and on the billboard, there it is. That would not be a pretty thing, would it?

"Let no one say,"

This is what James says.

Jas 1:13 "Let no one say when he is tempted, 'I am tempted from God;' for God is incapable of being tempted by what is evil and he himself tempts no one."

Jas 1:14 "But every person is tempted when he is drawn away, enticed and baited by his own evil desire, by his own lust, by his own passions."

Jas 1:15 "Then the evil desire, when it has conceived, gives birth to sin, and sin, when it is fully matured, brings forth death."

You need to be aware and willing to admit that all of your thoughts are not pure. All of your thoughts are not holy. You think some bad thoughts sometimes. It's a good thing that you don't act on them.

Jas 4:7 "Submit yourselves therefore to YeHoVaH. Resist the devil, and he will..."

Do what? This is a constant thing. There is a constant resisting because stuff is coming at us all of the time. It is constant. We are having thoughts all the time, even in conversations. Some of us have conversations with our spouse telepathically.

"Why are you looking like that? What did you just think? Oh, I saw it! What was on your mind?"

Do you ever have those kinds of conversations?

"What do you think? A penny for your thoughts."

"Why are you looking like that?"

Sometimes we are having some knock-down, drag-out fights in our mind and we don't even realize that our body is just going through the motions. Somebody is sitting there watching us, and it's like (looks around).

I pulled up to a car last week and there was this woman. She was driving. She stopped at the red light. And she had these scissors. She was just (makes cutting motions). She's just cutting her hair at the red light. Then it dawned on her that you know, she didn't have darkened windows in her car. She looked over and I'm like (looks at her). She burst out laughing, right? She rolled the window down and she said to me,

"Just trying to get rid of these split ends."

She rolled the window back up and we drove off laughing. Did you ever pull up to somebody and they're (drumming moves). They're beating drums! I mean (guitar moves, bobs head). We are going through the motions and we don't even know that we are making certain motions and movements; and showing certain looks on our face and responding to things that people who are watching us would wonder,

"What in the world is going on with that person?"

Thoughts. Whatsoever a man thinks, so is he.

1 Pe 5:6   "Humble yourselves therefore under the mighty hand of God, that he
might exalt you in due time:"

1 Pe 5:7   "Casting all your cares upon
him; for he cares for you."

Now we're talking about hearing the voice of
YeHoVaH. But what I'm trying to do is give you a
foundation to help you get to a point where you're going to
start recognizing some things, because all of this is part of
it. The Father cares for you.

1 Pt 5:8   "Be   sober,   be   vigilant;
because your adversary the devil, as a
roaring lion, walketh about, seeking whom
he may devour:"

One of the things that Christianity did is that it
debunked the devil. The focus became God — Jesus Christ,
grace, faith. But make no mistake about it folks, we've got
an enemy. That's not to be devil conscious, but you need to
know your enemy. You need to know how he operates.
You see, I figured out some time ago that we as human
beings respond certain ways to certain information and
certain thoughts.

Did you ever notice someone when they get bad news?
Have you ever seen someone who picks up the phone and
someone says something, and their response to what
happens on the phone stops you dead in your tracks? Now
your ears are in tune to another conversation.

We are so sensitive to our environment; to sound and
voices. Not all voices get to us, but certain things just take
our attention, just like that. The enemy watches you and I,
you see. Now you may think that nobody sees you — at
least nobody you know. This is why I say to brothers and

sisters, because it's not just the brothers and the sisters. It's not just the brothers who watch women's rear ends.

Women do it too now. Maybe they've always done it and we just didn't pay attention. But I think back to the Jordache blue jeans days and the Calvin Klein days when they used to make those commercials, you know?

The point is, sometimes when no one is around or sometimes when we are in a different city, or sometimes when we are on vacation, or sometimes when we are watching TV by ourselves, or sometimes when we are doing things and we think that we are in the comfort of our own presence and no one else is around, if we're not careful, we'll allow ourselves to do things that we wouldn't allow ourselves to do when someone else is around; especially our spouse. Does that look familiar to anybody?

Do you follow me? Now here is the thing folks. We may not necessarily know that we have an enemy. Those who are chess players, poker players, you know, you hear the term "poker face"? You have your face where your opponent can't read your next move. Some people are masters at reading your next move and setting you up so that you will be defeated — Checkmate. Do you hear what I'm saying?

The enemy Satan is a master chess player on the chessboard of life. He watches you. He observes your moves. He observes your eyes, your facial expressions. You see, the devil doesn't know what you are thinking, but he watches your response to certain things that are in your periphery. And once he watches your response, now he can begin to determine your move.

When he sees the areas of your weaknesses, he has a way of sending those things that he has identified as a weakness of yours across your path at critical times in your life for the sole purpose of entrapping or ensnaring, or bringing you down.

Your enemy the serpent is going about seeing whomever he can devour. And if you don't take control of your thoughts; pulling down strongholds, casting down imaginations, every high thing that exalts itself against the knowledge of YeHoVaH, you can't allow yourself to just go off in your thoughts.

That is because while you are going off in your thoughts, what you may not know is that the vision or what you are thinking about is a fiery dart of the enemy that has been lodged in your peripheral spirit. It causes you to now go down a path while he's writing out your expressions; your moves.

Now you don't know that. You think that because you're away from people; you're not at church, you're away from your husband, or you're away from your wife, or you're away from your boyfriend or your girlfriend, or your accountability partner, that you can just let your mind go. You can grin. You can smile. Your facial expressions are a dead giveaway.

The enemy is just taking notes. Mm hmm, Mm hmm. Oh, you've got an ambition to be a minister? You do? Wonderful, I like that, but you like looking at the ladies, don't you? Mm hmm, all right. Well, we're going to give you a big church! Yes we are. We're going to give you a gift where you can stand up and just mesmerize people with your voice and your moves and have the women swaying and swooning.

Just when you get to the pinnacle of your ministry, he sends Miss Secretary, Miss Administrative Assistant, Miss Elder's Wife who's got some issues because her husband doesn't satisfy her. She needs some counsel. She needs you to come over to her house and give her some counsel while the husband is at a Deacon's meeting. Do you follow what I'm saying?

A lot of men have been brought down because they didn't master passion, lust — and it's not just sex. It's

36

money, power, it's recognition. If you don't deal with these things that are in you — the Father is trying to get you to deal with them, just like He tried to get Cain to deal with the issues that were in him.

If you've got a Bible, I want you to turn to *Genesis* chapter number four, it says in verse number eight. In *Genesis* four, in verse eight. After YeHoVaH has this conversation with Cain; verse eight, the Bible says,

"And Cain talked with his brother."

Now that's a powerful statement. We don't know what they talk about. But because we have a tendency to read like English people, we assume that with the next statement, he talks with his brother. Then the Bibles says,

"And it came to pass"

This means that from the conversation that Cain has with his brother, to the time that he murders his brother, there is some distance between the conversation and the actual murder.

Is it possible that when Father convicted Cain about his attitude — because the Bible says that Cain — his offering was rejected. But the Father had respect for his, for Abel's offering. Is Cain watching? You know, I'm dancing in front of you saying,

"Look at me. Look at me."

And you are fixed on Abel.

"Why won't you look at me? Oh, you like Abel better than you like me, is that it?"

It's possible that Cain has some issues toward his brother. Father has a conversation with him. It is very possible that Cain now goes to his brother, apologizes; acknowledges the issues that he had, made amends, but didn't let it go. You see, there are times when we go

37

through and apologize and talk about how we forgive and all of that, but we don't let things go.

The moment that person does something, then all that stuff that we never let go is piled right back on top of this incident. You know this because here it is you forgave somebody. They do something else and in the discourse of telling them what they just did, you now go back and pull all that junk up that they did before and throw that in the mix.

> "See, I forgave you, but you ain't changed. Just like you did such and such, and such and such. So here you are doing it again."

> "Now wait a minute. I thought you forgave me for that."

> "I did until you did this."

> "So you stopped forgiving me?"

How often shall we forgive our brother? Do you see the deceitfulness of the heart? We say we forgive, but we still hold onto stuff. Cain here probably went and got things right with his brother, but then it came to pass. That is because Abel was bent on satisfying his Father.

Those of you who are bent on satisfying your Father in Heaven, guess what people are going to say to you? Guess what people are going to say about you? Yeah, your biological brother.

> "Oh, you think you are better than us now? Oh, you've arrived now. Oh, here it is you think you've got the truth now. Oh, oh, oh."

> **1 Pe 5:10-11** "But the God of all grace, who has called us unto his eternal glory by Messiah Yeshua, after that you have suffered a while, make you perfect,

stablish, strengthen, settle you. To him be glory and dominion forever and ever. Amen."

Part 2 Introduction:

This message is really dear to me because it is the voice of the Almighty that has brought me to where I am today. Those who have developed a relationship with Him and have learned to hear His voice know how critical it is to move when He says to move. I said this before. It's certainly worth repeating. If Fathers tells you to be here and you are over there, how many of you know that you are in the wrong place?

That's a dangerous place to be because if He is trying to get us to go to a particular place, that means that He is trying to get us away from where we might be. You never know. Where you might be, there might be one of those plane engines just falling out of the sky randomly on the very spot that you are on.

I mean, there are millions and millions of acres on the earth and you just so happen to be in the very spot that the engine is going to hit. Now what is the chance of something like that happening? It is probably one in a trillion, but it does happen.

Part 2 Teaching:

Ministers for too long have made things so easy to the point where people have gotten lazy. Instead of searching the scriptures to see what they say, people want to ask the preacher for a quick answer. Let me tell you something. If you get a quick answer, it's easy come, easy go. But when you spend the time to research and to study, that word sticks with you.

The Father has shown me; and we are going to get into this a little bit more today. Sometimes the Father will call somebody to ask a question just to get you into searching the scriptures. The question may have absolutely nothing to do with what the Father is trying to communicate. But He uses that to get you into the scriptures. And in the process of searching, He shows you things that you weren't even looking for — but He's answering questions that you have been praying about.

What He is trying to do is to get us into His word. Why? Because He and His word are one. When you get into the word, that is just like going into Father's bedroom and spending time talking to Him. That's what it is like. Just studying the word — asking questions going in with an open heart, an open mind and an open spirit — saying,

> "Father I am going to read this word. I don't have to understand what I am reading, but I know that through what you are going to speak to me and spending time in this book which contains the word of YeHoVaH..."

When you spend time in His word, you are spending time with Him. It is going to be critical if you ever desire or want or will come to a place where you hear His voice on a regular basis. That's one of the main ways in which He speaks.

When I look at where I came from, I see the things that I have done in my life that disqualify me (by all natural accounts) to even contemplate; to consider preaching and teaching and praying and believing. You know when I look at where I've come from and I see where Father has me, it is a very humbling place. This is because in essence, none of us are qualified.

I say this for those of you out there who don't feel that you may be qualified or called. Every believer is called as an ambassador and as a minister — and encouraging people who think,

> "I don't know what to say. I don't know what to do. I don't know enough of the scripture."

Well, share what you do know. This is another avenue of where when we are faithful over the little — if all you know is:

> "God so loved the world,"

Then share that. Do you hear what I'm saying? If you are passionate about sharing that, Father looks and says,

> "You know, there is a passionate one. Let me give them a little bit more because I know that if I give them something, they are not going to keep it to themselves."

There are too many of His people keeping what He has shared with them to themselves. He says,

> "They are not going to do anything with it. Why would I waste my time downloading into them when they are just going to keep it to themselves?"

But when you are passionate and you are faithful in the little, He says,

> "What I reveal to you in secret, you shout it from the mountain; or you shout it from the rooftop."

There needs to be a lot more rooftop shouting folks. Do you hear what I'm saying? When we are diligent about the little, He begins to pour out more and more.

If you missed the teaching I did on **Maximizing Your Talents**, I'm telling you, that's one of those messages that says to you that you use what the Father has given you. If you use what He has given you and you use it wisely, then what you will find is that He is going to add more and more and more to you.

We believe that we've got a message to share. We are going to do everything within our power to get it out there as far and as wide as we can.

(Prayer & Shema)

Yesterday some interesting things happened. I was standing at a window of my house and looking out at the backyard and I saw this strange sight. There was this bird doing something that I had never seen before. This sparrow is what it looked like, flew up and flew down. It flew up. It flew down. It flew up and it flew down again. Those of you who have watched these humming birds, you can see that they do that kind of stuff. But this sparrow did this, and then he darted to a tree, to another tree, and then to another branch and then he left. So I'm there pondering that.

Last night as I'm sleeping, I am having this strange type of sleep where I am asleep but I'm awake. And while I'm sleeping, I'm watching myself being awake, and watching myself being asleep.

Now I'm thinking, you know, this is weird. Then I go into this dream. In this dream, the house that I am in (and I am there), there are hundreds of sparrows in the house. They are all different colors and there are nests everywhere. I am thinking,

"Where did these things come from?"

Then I look over and there are what look like holes in the room and what look like colorful lizards looking at me. Then the lizards fly, but they weren't lizards. They were sparrows — at least I thought they were sparrows.

So I woke up this morning and I'm preparing today. All of a sudden the dream comes back to me. While I was in the dream, I looked for a broom because I'm going to get all of those sparrows out of my house. I'm gonna knock the nests down. There are nests sitting and there are nests hanging. I've never really seen hanging nests, but that's what I'm seeing. I noticed as I was trying to shoo the birds out, they were sitting there looking at me like,

"What are you doing?"

I am thinking,

"This is strange. Why is the bird looking at me like, 'What are you doing?'"

As I was pondering this this morning, this is what I believe the Father spoke to me. I am wondering why are these birds here? I got up after this, and Father said,

"The reason why the birds where there is because of the seeds — the word — there's food. The birds have found food, and you're not going to get rid of them. They are coming from all over the place."

This led me to go and now I'm sitting at my Bible. The Father leads me to *Psalm* 84. This is what it says:

Ps 84:1-2 "How amiable are thy tabernacles, O YeHoVaH of hosts! My soul longeth, yea, even fainteth for the courts of YeHoVaH: my heart and my flesh cry out for the living God."

Ps 84:3   "Yea, the sparrow has found
an house, and the swallow a nest,"

I go to the dictionary because I recognized the sparrow. But the lizard-looking flying things I never recognized. They were swallows. I looked up "swallow" and swallows burrow. Their nests are very different because they live in sand dunes. They live in holes. So here it is in this place that the sparrow and the swallow have accumulated themselves. This is what it says:

"...and the swallow a nest for herself, where
she may lay her young,"

In the nests there were little babies and they were being fed by the big birds. It says,

"...she may lay her young, even thine altars,
O YeHoVaH of hosts, my King, and my God."

Now in another verse, it says that the sparrow and the swallow live in the place next to the altar. In other words, they make their nests. They made their nests in the temple. This is what they are doing. And what the Father was showing is that, listen. Even though there are times — you see, nobody can be hard on me; harder on me than I am on myself.

What the Father was saying to us is that we are doing the work. We are feeding people from all over the globe. And what He said is that these birds are representative of the people that you are reaching.

Now I am looking at sparrows and there are like fifteen species of sparrows in the United States. The swallows and the sparrows are indigenous to six of the seven continents. Then I went on *YouTube* and I started looking at the analytics of from where people are joining us. And do you know that there are seven continents? We have people on all seven continents that are joining us in our services because of the word. They are looking for food. They are looking to be fed. They are looking for meat.

In this case, it is interesting that sparrows eat seed. The seed is the word. The sower sows the seed. Now I'm not the kind of person — those of you who know me, this is probably the first time I've ever started the message out concerning a dream. I don't deal. I don't get into those aspects. But when the Father is in something, I have to take note of it. And what He is saying to us is that,

> "Listen. We are making such a difference and such an impact in people's lives all over the globe."

I'm sitting there at my computer choked up because as I continue to read that, He says:

> **Ps 84:3** "Yea, the sparrow has found an house, and the swallow a nest for herself,"

And here it is I'm trying to get rid of these sparrows and get them out of my house because it is like they are all over the place. But they are there because there is food. Look at the next few verses.

> **Ps 84:4** "Blessed are they that dwell in thy house: they will be still praising thee. Selah."

> **Ps 84:5-6** "Blessed is the man whose strength is in thee; in whose heart are the ways of them. Who passing through the valley of Baca make it a well; the rain also filleth the pools."

> **Ps 84:7-8** "They go from strength to strength; every one of them in Zion

appeareth before Elohim. O YeHoVaH God of hosts, hear my prayer: give ear, O God of Jacob. Selah."

Ps 84:11-12   "For YeHoVaH God is a sun and shield: YeHoVaH will give grace and glory: no good thing will he withhold from them that walk uprightly. O YeHoVaH of hosts, blessed is the man that trusteth in thee."

There seems to be a verse that is missing here. There is. I don't know how in the world I did that because it's verse ten. *Psalms* 84, verse number ten. It really speaks to my heart and I know it speaks to the heart of so many others. This is what it says:

Ps 84:10   "For a day in your courts is better than a thousand. I had rather be a doorkeeper in the house of Elohim than to dwell in the tents of wickedness."

So many times I remember saying,

"You know, I am just glad that I am in the house. You know, I am so glad that I'm a part of what the Father is doing. I don't have to be up front. I'm just glad to be in the house."

Do you hear what I am saying? And the psalmist says,

"I would rather be a doorkeeper in the house of YeHoVaH..."

That's powerful.

"...than to dwell in the tents of wickedness."

Ps 84:11-12 "For YeHoVaH God is a sun and shield: YeHoVaH will give grace and glory: no good thing will he withhold from them that walk uprightly. O YeHoVaH of hosts, blessed is the man that trusteth in thee."

This Psalm speaks so much to me that you know, when I really think about the whole idea of trusting — because I had to come to a place like many of you. I had to be honest with myself. You know we can tell people,

> "Yeah, I trust God. Yeah, I trust God. Yeah, I trust God."

Nobody knows your thoughts. Nobody knows what you think about when you are faced with issues that the Father is saying,

> "Do you trust me?"

How much we want to take things into our own hands. How much we want to make our own way. How much we want to fix a situation or fix a person. How much we talk about praying for somebody but then,

> "God is not moving fast enough, so we've got to help him out."

You see when we trust the Almighty, we literally back up and say,

> "Father you've got this. I'm just going to watch you work. And whatever the outcome of this situation is, I accept it because I know that you know what's best for me."

I think I know what's best for me, but I don't know. I really don't know. There are things that I thought I wanted, and once I got it, it's not what I wanted. There are some things — you've heard people say,

> "Be careful what you ask for, you just might get it. Be careful what you pray for, you just might get it."

And yet the Father is bringing us to a place. It is like, what has this got to do with how to hear His voice? You see, a major part of walking with the Father is trusting Him to know better for you than you think you know for yourself. Let me tell you something, every one of you. I can look in your eyes, and you think you are pretty smart — every one of you.

You've got a better way of doing anything that somebody else is doing. You've got your way of doing it, which is opposed to maybe the way somebody else is doing it. You want to one-up. Did you ever hear of somebody who is telling a story, and it's like you know, let me tell you what happened to me? Well you know that's nothing. Let me tell you about my situation.

As human beings, that's the way we are — that's our nature. The Father is saying,

> "Do you really trust me?"

This really struck home to me one day I was in Michigan and I was on my face prostrate before the Father. My mouth was moving. I was going through the ritual, even to the point of prostrating on the ground; on the floor talking to Him. Meanwhile my mind was going through my Franklin planner and all the appointments that I had to do and the things that I had to get done.

Right there in the midst of while I was praying and talking to Him, what the Father showed me was,

> "Listen. Your mouth — you are honoring me, but your heart is someplace else. You

are talking to me. Your lips are moving. Words are coming out of your mouth. But what is in your heart is what you have to get done today."

How often do we go through life and we talk to God for a few minutes and then leave Him in the prayer closet? We go out and close the door.

"I'll see you in a little bit. Don't go anywhere because I expect you to be there when I get back."

Father is screaming,

"I want to go! I want to go with you! I want to order your steps. I want to lead you. I want to guide you. I want to show you. I want to navigate your path!"

This is what I believe the Bible means when we are told to pray without ceasing — to always be in tune, to always be in communication with the Father. How is He going to order your steps if we are not hearing Him — if we are not listening — if we don't know what He sounds like? We tell God what we want.

"Father this is what I need. I need a husband. I need a wife. I need a job. I need a car. I need this, I need that. I need that. Father bless me with this, bless me with that."

Father says,

"What you need is me. What you NEED is ME. Seek first MY Kingdom; MY righteousness, and all that other stuff will be added."

But no, it's I need this! You give me that, I'll seek you. You give me that, I'll do that. You do this for me, and I'll do that for you. Father says,

> "That's not how it works. I'm looking to establish a relationship with you. Why? Because there are some things that I want to show you about yourself."

Many of us, we believe the lies. We believe the bad things that people have said about us. We've let people talk down to us. We've let people cause us to think we're crazy. We've let people cause us to think that we've lost our minds. We're insane. We're a good for nothing, nothing. We deserve all the stuff that we are getting.

Then we come to a place where many people believe the lies of the enemy; which causes them not to trust the Father with their very life. And the Father is saying,

> "You can trust Me. I'm not going to hurt you. I'm not going to leave you. I'm not going to forsake you. I will get you to where I want you to go because where you think you want to go is not really where you need to be."

As we shared last week, from *Genesis* to *Revelation* we see that Yah is speaking. The Bible opens up in *Genesis* one verse 3a where it says:

Gen 1:3a   "Then God said."

Revelation closes with:

"The Spirit and the bride say."

Throughout biblical history, believers and non-believers alike have heard the voice of God. Adam and Eve along with their murdering son Cain all heard the creator's voice.

Prophets, Kings, Pharaohs, and even the common working man had encounters and were given direction directly from YeHoVaH's mouth. Moses said:

Dt 8:3   "He humbled you,"

The question then becomes:

> "He humbled you, causing you to hunger and then feeding you with manna, which neither you nor your fathers had known,"

He's talking with Moses and Moses is speaking this to the people. He says:

> "To teach you that man does not live on bread alone, but on every word that comes from the mouth of YeHoVaH."

Yeshua said:

Mt 4:4   "It is written:"

He is quoting the prophet; quoting Moses:

> "Man does not live on bread alone, but on every word that comes from the mouth of God."

What I'm looking for — even I read the scriptures, I'm looking for the words that came from the mouth of YeHoVaH to His servants, the prophets. I'm looking for what comes from His mouth. Yeshua came and said that he didn't come to abolish the Law or the prophets — that the word of YeHoVaH is for us today.

We've got to identify and learn how He speaks to us, where He speaks to us, what is He saying to us, and what is He asking us to do? Chances are, He's asking us to do some stuff we don't want to do. It's not in our plan or our agenda. Yeshua also said:

Jn 10:2-3 "But he that entereth in by the door is the shepherd of the sheep. To him the porter openeth; and the sheep hear his voice: and he calleth his own sheep by name, and leadeth them out."

Jn 10:4-5 "And when he putteth forth his own sheep, he goeth before them, and the sheep follow him: for they know his voice. And a stranger will they not follow, but will flee from him: for they know not the voice of strangers."

Here is the question ladies and gentlemen. Why does YeHoVaH communicate with His people? Why does He want you to hear His voice?

This is what Moses said in *Deuteronomy* 4:33 and following:

Dt 4:33 "Did ever people hear the voice of God speaking out of the midst of the fire, as you heard, and live?"

I want to stop here for just a moment because as I continue to read this; as I continue to study, I look at the words of the Torah and think about the awesomeness of what happened at Mount Sinai. It is one time in history that we know of, that we can literally point to scripture and say that every Israelite; every person who came out of Egypt following the Almighty simultaneously all at once heard His voice — every last one of them.

The Father is speaking and there is not a creature alive in the midst of them that does not hear the voice — every one of them. That's the plan that the Father laid out. Bring the people. I want to introduce Myself to them. I want to speak to them. I want to have a relationship with them. I want them to know My voice so I can distinctly; orderly move them from where they are to where they need to go.

It was not the Father's plan for Moses to be a mediator; not originally. Even at creation, everybody heard the voice. Adam heard it. Eve heard it. The serpent heard it. The trees heard it. All the animals heard it.

"Adam! Where are you?"

Everybody heard. You see, the Father desires all of His people to hear His voice; to know what He sounds like, to follow His instructions.

> **Dt 4:34**   "Or has God ever tried to go and take for Himself a nation from the midst of another nation, by trials, by signs, by wonders, by war, by a mighty hand, by an outstretched arm, and by great terrors, as YeHoVaH your God did for you in Egypt before your eyes?"

Moses is saying to the Israelites,

> "Let me tell you something folks. You all are history in the making."

In other words, the Father at this particular juncture in time decides that He's going to choose a people. He does something He has never done in history before — a whole people. Of course He said Noah and his sons and their wives — but an entire people to establish a nation. He says,

> "It's never been done before."

> **Dt 4:35**   "To you it was shown, that you might realize and have personal knowledge"

You see, Father doesn't want you believing in Him because of what somebody else said. His relationship with you is not based upon your mom's relationship with Him or your dad's relationship with Him; or your uncle, or your brother or your sister. He desires to know YOU.

> **Dt 4:35**   "To you it was shown, that you might realize and have personal knowledge that YeHoVaH is God;"

Remember the woman at the well? The woman at the well has an encounter with Yeshua. He tells her about herself. She goes back into the city. The next thing you know, she's brought the city out. The people said,

> "Do you know what? We heard what the woman said, but now we know for ourselves."

You see, ministry, evangelism — why we're talking about preaching, reaching and teaching, is to bring the message of truth to people. It is not that we can be a mediator between them and the Father. Our goal is to make the connection. My job is to get out of the way, but people want to keep me in the midst.

Effective ministry is to tell you what YeHoVaH says, to connect you to Him, and then allow Him to lead you. Otherwise, people will get in the way. And guess what? Your human nature prefers there to be a person between you and the Almighty. Now I don't care what you say with your mouth, because I know humans. I know the nature. Do you know how I know it? When you have a question, you ask somebody else before you ask Him.

People get sick. They'll call a doctor sometimes before they call the Father. They'll call on somebody to pray for them before they ask the Father to heal them. They'll seek for mediators. They'll seek for answers. They'll seek for someone to intercede.

> "Oh, I'm just calling all of the prayer
> warriors because I need to get a prayer
> through. And I need you to put my name..."

Now I'm not mocking anybody folks. I'm just calling it like it is. Sometimes that gets me in trouble because people hear and they say,

> "He's talking about me."

Well, I'm talking about you. We're not going to hide that fact today. I'm talking about all of "yous," okay? We have a tendency to call.

> "Okay, put me on the prayer list. Put me on
> that prayer list. I need the intercessors to
> pray."

Okay, how much time have you spent talking to Him? Let me tell you something about Father. If there's an issue in your life that He needs to intervene, the first thing that He wants to do is to get a hold of you to show you, *you*. But because we're human beings — and let me tell you something. Every last one of you; every last one of us has an addictive personality. We just may not be addicted to the same things.

Every one of us has something that comforts us other than the comforter. And we seek that comforter for comfort when we need comfort instead of getting in the presence of the Almighty and allowing Him to deal with us. Now let me tell you something about addictive behavior, because I know a little bit about addictive behavior. I was an addict for a lot of years. I was an addict on everything, you see.

There's something about addictive behavior that keeps a person in a pattern of addiction. Do you know what that is? Reality. Reality is painful. When we think about what has to be done — when we think about what needs to be done and that we're the person for the job, sometimes that's a painful reality, especially when we're looking at situations. We're looking at our lives. We see the messes that we've made and we find ourselves at the center of the mess. It's easier to blame someone else for our problems than it is to blame ourselves. That's an addictive personality.

The moment you begin to shift the blame to somebody else for what you are experiencing right now, is a person who is not ready to deal with reality. But regardless of how you got here, what are you going to do to get out of it?

So when we get into the presence of the Father, the Father starts showing us stuff about ourselves that we don't like. He wants to deal with us, but we want Him to deal with somebody else. Now Father wants to talk about me. I want Him to do this over here. He's trying to get me to do stuff. I mean, we've had that conversation before. I wasn't going to do it then and I'm not doing it now. Some of us don't actually say that. Our actions say that. He wanted to show you:

> **Dt 4:35-36**   "that you might realize and have personal knowledge that YeHoVaH is God; there is no other besides Him. Out of heaven He made you hear His voice,"

Now notice, Moses is talking to the children of Israel. He says,

> "Now, every last one of you heard His voice."

But what was your response?

> "Don't talk to us."

Talk to my agent. Talk to my pastor. Talk to my husband. Talk to my wife. Talk to my boss. Don't talk to me.

"...that He might correct,"

Do you see this?

Dt 4:36　　　"Out of heaven He made you hear His voice, that He might correct,"

"...that He might discipline,"

"...that He might admonish you;"

These are all painful words to the flesh. Correction is not good when it comes. I mean it's not pleasant, as it says. Father wants to correct us. We want Him to fix something. He wants to correct us because He knows. Okay, I can fix that, but because of the condition you are in — I mean, after all, even though you are blaming somebody for the mess over there, if you don't get fixed, you'll just make the mess somewhere else. That is because you are messy and mess will follow you. Now if you want the mess to stop, let Me clean up the mess — and the mess is you.

When He gets in our face, I mean you know, it's like we don't want to hear what He has to say because I don't think we're going to like what He's going to say. Habakkuk had to get to a place where he says,

> "Listen. You know, I need to prepare myself because I'm about to go in here and have a conversation with the Almighty. I know He's going to say some stuff. So let me get my pencil, let me get my — well he probably didn't have a pencil. Let me get my writing utensils, and I'm going to sit here on my watch and I'm going to wait, so that when He speaks, I'm going to write it down."

He didn't trust his mind to hear what the Father said. He says,

"I'm going to write it down."

He knew that if he put himself in a position where Father would speak, He was going to speak.

The society and the world that we live in continues to bombard us and to make us busy with all kinds of stuff. You are busy, busy, busy doing nothing. What I'm doing is important. Yes, it is important. But is it as important as hearing the voice of the Father? Let me tell you something. One word from Him and it changes everything — just one word. He can change your circumstance in just a moment.

Some of you heard. We had a neighbor. The neighbor was making life miserable for us. I mean, we've got a room back there that has a door that swings both ways. This guy — he put these big old heavy tractor tires at the door so we couldn't get access to the sink; on purpose. I mean, this is the kind of stuff we dealt with. I'm in here contemplating.

> "Father, I just need heaven; I need lightning to strike this guy. I need You to do something. I need him to know that hey, I'm Your servant, and he can't mess with me like that."

And Father says,

> "Do you know what? Really, he's doing this because he thinks that you have disrespected him."

Now I'm searching my heart. I've not disrespected him.

> "Okay, well what do I do?"

> "Apologize."

> "Apologize for what?"

> "Apologize for disrespecting him."

"I didn't disrespect him."

"It doesn't matter what you think, that's what he thinks."

You see, when a person is fixed in their mind that something is a certain way, you can spend your life trying to convince them that it is not that way. But they've already come to the conclusion that that's the way it is. So this is not going to be one of those five and dime apologies.

"Hey, listen. IF I offended you in any way, please forgive me."

Now the Father says,

"The man thinks you disrespected him."

So I go over to him, and I said,

"Listen man. I apologize for disrespecting you."

I said those very words. Do you know at that very moment, that person who was my sworn enemy became an advocate? He went from adversary to advocate, all from an apology that I gave that I didn't believe I owed.

But it didn't matter what I believed. It's what He said. Do you see what I'm saying? One word from Him and it just changed the entire environment around here. One word from Him will change your house. One word from Him will change your spouse. Do you hear what I'm saying? So what we have to do is we have to get out of the way; get into His presence, let Him speak to us, and then do what He says to do. Because what's the point of Him speaking to you if you are not going to obey it? That's why we do the Shema every Sabbath.

"Hear and obey."

It's not just something nice to do. The word of YeHoVaH is about to come and the word of YeHoVaH is going to speak to your heart. He's going to give you some instructions and He's going to show you something that you need to do. You need to write it down and then make haste to do it. That is because if you procrastinate, the enemy is going to come and circumstances and situations — you go out there and say,

"Oh man, I've got a flat."

All of a sudden, all of that information that you were storing in your brain gets dumped. You fix the flat and you're on your way home and here you go. Now God said something to me today. What was that? What was it that He said? Man. Anybody ever have one of those moments?

He spoke to you, but how do you take what He says? Is it something you take lightly? Most of us take the word, the voice of YeHoVaH very lightly. The way you know you haven't taken it lightly is that you do like the psalmist says. You do like the word says. You guard it. You GUARD it.

You do like Habakkuk says. You write it down. You write it down and you've got a record of it. It's not just in your mind, because the enemy is coming. Whenever the word of YeHoVaH is spoken; whenever the word is sown in your heart, the enemy is coming immediately to steal it. You can't trust your mind. I don't care how good your memory is.

You see, we remember a lot of useless stuff. We've got figures and numbers and formulas in our heads. But the word when it is sown — you see, the enemy is not coming to get that information you've got. He's coming to get the word. That's why a lot of you experience warfare; because it's the enemy coming to steal something from you. That's what he does. He says:

Dt 4:36   "Out of heaven He made you hear His voice."

He MADE you. The people weren't looking to hear the voice of YeHoVaH. He called them. He initiated the meeting. He says,

> "Moses, you tell the people that in three days I'm coming down. You get them ready. You tell them what to do, and I'm going to meet them. I want to meet with them. I want them to present themselves to Me."

This is what the book of *Romans* talks about — presenting your body as a living sacrifice. It is presenting ourselves — every Sabbath, every Feast day is a presentation. The day that He has set apart to meet with us, He is coming to meet with us and we are coming to meet with Him. That is the whole point of the *moedim*. It's an appointed time.

It is a time that He has set. And through us collectively gathering together where He is in the midst of us, He is coming to communicate to each and every one of us where we are. What you hear over here and back there and over here is going to be totally different. Through the words that I am speaking, the Holy Spirit is taking words that I am speaking.

He is taking a piece off for you; taking a piece off for you, and everybody is hearing — just like on the day of Pentecost, on Shavuot. As they were speaking in tongues, everybody was hearing in their own language, the wonderful works of YeHoVaH.

That's why I'm not surprised when people say,

> "You know, that message was just for me."
> "Well that message was just for me."

And if I asked you,

"Well, what part of the message was just for you?"

The reason I am asking you what part is because I'm trying to help seal it. How many times have we gone and you've heard people say,

"Man, that was a good message today."

That was a good service today? Okay, well what was said? What was said? People remember the experience because the adrenaline flows. They got happy. They got excited. There was joy. In the midst of all the adrenaline and all the joy and all the happiness and all the excitement and all of the being in the presence of other people, the word escapes. It doesn't go on its own. Something came. Somebody came to take it.

The whole purpose is that if it doesn't get sown into your heart, you will not apply it. If you don't apply it, you are a hearer and not a doer. If you are a hearer only, you deceive yourself. And if you are deceived, you will think you know, but don't know. You will have the head knowledge, but you won't walk it out.

You will continue to learn; continue to get information, but never come into the knowledge of truth. You see, it's the truth that makes you free, not just the information. It's when you get the truth, you apply the truth. You walk the truth and then you will see the Almighty who watches over that truth, bring it to pass. Having information is dangerous if you are not going to apply it. It is better for you not to know.

Why does He want us to hear His voice? He says,

"I made you."

He made you hear His voice because He wanted to correct you. You see, He's bringing them out of a way of doing things. Can you imagine? I know we can — we fall in love with the Ten Commandments and we see the outstretched hand of the Almighty.

But here is what we don't see. We don't see all the abuses each one of those Israelites and those strangers who left Egypt endured. We don't see their personal life. We don't see the Egyptian raping the wife or raping the daughter or beating the son. We don't see the injustices that each of these individuals experienced.

We see that they were in bondage. We see that they were mistreated. We see that they were abused, but we don't see the personal story of each of these people. Every last one of them had a personal issue; a personal story. All of them were slaves.

There was no such thing as good treatment for slaves in Egypt in the day. They were beaten. They were tortured. They were abused. They were denied basic rights. They had to make bricks without straw. I mean it was all kinds of stuff. As a people and as individuals; every last one of those Israelites had a story. That's why Father wanted them all to have a relationship — because they all had a story. He says,

> "I know your story. I know your story. I know your story. I KNOW your story. I KNOW your story. I KNOW your story. I know YOUR story. I've got the answer. But let me talk to you about you."

With every story there are deficiencies that are established as a result of what people go through. You see, every situation you experience causes you to adapt. And through adapting to circumstances, situations, problems, issues, abuses, disappointments, let-downs and being taken advantage of; we automatically through adaptation become something totally different than we were designed to be.

We have become lost in life. We have become lost in circumstances, lost in situations, lost in family issues, lost in female issues, lost in male issues, lost in identity issues. We suffer from an identity crisis. We all want to be ourselves, but we don't know who we are. So now we want you to respect me. We want you to treat me right. We don't want you to "dis" (disrespect) me.

> "Who do you think you are talking to? You don't know who I am."

Do you? Do you know who you are? Because chances are, you don't. If you think you do and you call yourself a believer, understand that your true identity is hidden in Messiah. This means that even though you think that you know who you are, you still have to die to you.

Many of us have been "almost" left for dead. Life has beaten many of us up. If you grew up in a home town where I grew up, you swore that the first chance you got, you were getting up out of there. If you grew up in a house like I grew up in, all you could think about was running away.

If you grew up in a school that I grew up in, all you saw were people teasing people. You thought about your future and what you were going to be. You think about what you said you were going to be when you were young. Now that you're old, you look at what you've become. You ask yourself,

> "Am I where I am supposed to be? Is this part of the plan that I set for my life? Did I settle? Did I go with the program? Did I not rock the boat when I should have rocked the boat? Did I go along with the situations that I shouldn't have gone along with?"

All of that history is what brought you to where you are. All of that history caused you to think about yourself the way you think about yourself. And many of you, if you are anything like me, you are pretty hard on yourself.

Father says,

> "I've got a better plan. You see, because I LOVE you more than you love you. I KNOW the plans that I have for you. But I've got to get you out of the way before I reveal My plan to you. That is because if I reveal My plan to you the way you are, you're just going to mess it up too."

You are messy. Now I'm not preaching at you folks, I'm just telling you. Father says,

"I made you to hear My voice."

Why?

> "Because I need to correct you. I need to discipline you. I need to admonish you."

> **Dt 4:36-37** "...and on earth He made you see His great fire, and you heard His words out of the midst of the fire, Because he loved your ancestors, chose their descendants after them and brought you out of Egypt with his presence and great power,"

I know for a fact and I have to believe this. I knew my mom and dad. I knew my grandfather on my mother's side. I didn't know my grandfather or grandmother on my father's side. I have no idea what their parents were like.

But here is what I have to believe. I have to believe that somewhere back in my family tree, somebody had a right relationship with the Father. I have to believe that. I have to believe that because of where I am today.

You see, I was on the same track as everybody else in my family. And throughout all of our lives, I know the Father has been trying to get our attention. Some of us are easier to get a hold of than others. Some of us are just flat-out hard-headed. My parents used to say to me all the time,

"Boy, a hard head makes a soft behind."

That's what they used to say. I had a hard head, a thick skull. You know the more I think about it, maybe Alpha (Arthur's son) does take after me, because I was a hard-headed "scound-booger" (urban slang). I was a mischievous, hard-headed, devious little fellow who could charm Mama. Oh, I was a charmer. Do you know what I'm saying? Oh yeah. I was a charmer, but I didn't even realize that I had some Cain brothers and sisters. I was Abel. They tell me stories.

"You know, you had Mama wrapped around your finger, just like that."

"I did?"

"Yes you did."

Anyway, because He loved your ancestors is what He's saying. Somebody in your tree somewhere is the reason why you are where you are today. Here is what I intend. If the Father — if Yeshua tarries, I intend to be the marker for my family going forward. If he tarries for another 2, 3, 4, 5, 6 generations, even though my great-great-great-great-great-great-great grandson may not know who I am, they will be blessed as a result of the stand that I am taking right now.

You can stop the madness today. Whatever the madness has been; whatever house you were brought up in, whatever circumstances you were born in, you can stop the madness today. Or you can continue to make the excuses that you are in the condition that you are in because of your parents, because of the city you grew up in, because of the house you grew up in, because of all the stuff that happened to you.

Every last one of those Israelites had a story. And when Father brought them to the foot of that mountain, He said,

> "Listen. I AM. I AM your everything. I AM all you need. I know what you need and I have already supplied your needs. I've got a place for you. As a matter of fact, before I came and got you out of Egypt, I've already prepared a place for you. And it's a land flowing with milk and honey, with houses you didn't build; wells you didn't dig, olive trees you didn't plant. I did all of that because of the promise I made to your ancestors. And I watch over My word."

You see. The Bible says:

> "He remembered His promise."

He is not a forgetful God!

Dt 4:37 "Because he loved your ancestors, chose their descendants after them and brought you out of Egypt with his presence and great power..."

"...And because He loved your fathers, He chose their descendants after them, and brought you out from Egypt with His own Presence, by His mighty power."

67

Dt 4:38 "Driving out nations from before you, greater and mightier than yourselves,"

I mean when you think about it, the Father — man, this is why it is so important for us to develop that relationship because He goes before us. He is our rear guard. He is encamped all about us. He is a high tower. He watches over us while we sleep. He says:

Dt 4:38 "Driving out nations from before you, greater and mightier than yourselves, to bring you in, to give you their land for an inheritance, as it is this day;"

Dt 4:39 "Know, recognize, and understand therefore this day and turn your [mind and] heart to it that YeHoVaH is God in the heavens above and upon the earth beneath; there is no other."

Dt 4:40 "Therefore you shall keep His statutes and His commandments, which I command you this day, that it may go well with you and your children after you..."

Now what He's saying,

"and your children after you,"

This is your children, your children's children, your children's children's children, your children's children's children's children.

"...and that you may prolong your days in the land which YeHoVaH your God gives you forever."

Then there are these Psalms (*Psalms* 95:1-11). For this one, I just want us to — I want to encourage you to bring your Bibles, because from time to time we are going to read. I want to get to a certain place and it looks like we may not get there, but we'll get as far as we can. *Psalms* 95:

> "Oh come, let us sing unto YeHoVaH. Let us make a joyful noise to the rock of our salvation. Let us come before His presence with thanksgiving. And make a joyful noise unto Him with psalms."

Do you know, no matter what you are going through, no matter where you are — I try to visualize as you have heard me say before. You will hear me saying some of the same stuff over and over and over and over again, because repetition is good; especially truth. We need to hear it over and over again. When I look at David I hear, I read David saying,

> "Bless the Lord."

I mean think about this.

> "Bless the Lord, Oh my soul."

Who is he talking to?

> "And all that is within me."

I believe that there are times in our lives when we are going through stuff; that we are feeling down, unworthy and undeserving — that we've got to make ourselves praise Him. We've got to force praise. I can see David going through this, probably because of something he did; saying,

> "Bless the Lord Oh my soul; all that is in me. Bless His holy name. For He has done GREAT things."

I mean I can imagine him having to work himself up to a place where he gets out of his flesh, into his spirit, cries out to the Almighty and the Almighty hears him from heaven.

There are times when we don't feel like praising Him. There are times when we don't feel like giving Him the worship that He is due. Every day I encourage you to start your day off with this:

"This is the day..."

Not just on the Sabbath.

"This is the day YeHoVaH has made. I WILL,
I WILL rejoice."

And let me just give you a pointer because I believe that the dream last night was from pondering the sparrow in my yard. Often times what you go to bed with on your mind is what is going to affect you during your sleep; and you are going to wake up with it.

This is why before you go to bed — let me just give you some pointers. You need to get some pleasant thoughts. The best thoughts to get are the thoughts of YeHoVaH. I'm preaching to myself in my sleep last night. I do it all the time; especially on Friday nights.

During the course of the night I'm ministering and preaching in my dream. Then I get up in the morning and I'm putting PowerPoints together, and I'm watching. As I'm looking at the scriptures that the Father is giving me, I'm sitting there getting all excited and getting all blessed. And I know that you know, this blessed me. People are going to get blessed by this message because I'm blessed by it, you see.

You've got to make yourself do things you don't want to do. When you don't feel like praising, that's the best time to praise. Somebody said there are two times to praise, and there are two times only to praise. When you feel like it and when you don't. It's not about how you feel. You have to make yourself praise Him. When you make yourself praise Him, you get out of yourself.

> **There are two times to praise YeHoVaH:**
> **When we feel like it, and when we don't!**

You've got this spirit that desires the things of the Spirit. But the flesh desires the things of the flesh. That's why when you feel down you want to be around down people. You don't want to be around excited people when you feel down. Did you ever notice that? The flesh doesn't like excited people when the flesh doesn't feel right. Misery loves company.

You get around a down person. They open their mouth and now their "downness" is dumped onto you. I get around a down person and I'm going to go to work to cheer them up. If they refuse to be cheered up,

"See ya."

I learned a long time ago, that God doesn't come to pity parties. He likes to party, but He doesn't like a pity party. He really doesn't. When you are done over there sulking and sobbing and talking about how:

"Woe is me,"

Then you call on me.

Ps 95:3-11 "For YeHoVaH is a great El, and a great King above all Elohims. In his hand are the deep places of the earth; the strength of the hills is his also, the sea is his, and he made it: and his hands formed the dry ground. O come, let us worship and bow down: let us kneel before YeHoVaH

71

our maker. For he is our Elohim; and we are the people of his pasture, and the sheep of his hand. To day if ye will hear his voice, Harden not your heart, as in the provocation, as of the day of temptation in the wilderness: When your fathers tempted me, proved me, and saw my work. Forty years long was I grieved with that generation, and said, it is a people that do err in their heart, and they have not known my ways: Unto whom I sware in my wrath that they should not enter into my rest."

The day you hear His voice — see, the day you are hearing His voice. I know you are. There are some things that are coming out and being spoken to you, and you know who you are. The Father is trying to get you to allow Him to come in and to bring the healing.

Some of you are afraid to be free because you have become used to bondage. You are afraid of laughing. You are afraid of enjoying life. You are afraid of being free and allowing the Holy Spirit to really move and manifest Himself in you.

You are afraid of what other people might say; what other people might think. You are afraid you might mess up. You might make a mistake. God hasn't given you a spirit of fear. *Hebrews* chapter three (*Hebrews* 3:7-11 and *Hebrews* 3:15-19) verse seven.

Heb 3:7-9 "Wherefore, as the Holy Spirit says, 'Today if you will hear His voice, harden not your hearts as in the provocation, in the day of temptation in the wilderness, when your fathers tempted me, proved me, and saw my works for forty years.'"

I mean you know, *Hebrews* is basically verbatim to *Psalms*. As I was saying on Thursday for Discipleship class, it is amazing that the book of *Hebrews* is in the Greek New Testament. Isn't that amazing? The book of *Hebrews* — translated from the Greek.

> **Heb 3:9**   "when your fathers tempted me, proved me, and saw my works for forty years."

Verse 10:

> "Wherefore I was grieved with that generation, and said, 'they do always err in their heart, and them not knowing my ways, so I swore, I swear in my wrath, they shall not enter into my rest.'"

And then, look at verse number 15:

> "While it is said, 'Today, if you will hear his voice, harden not your hearts, as in the day of provocation.' For some, when they had heard, did provoke. Howbeit not all that came out of Egypt by Moses; but with whom was he grieved forty years? Was it not with them that had sinned, whose carcasses fell in the wilderness? And to whom, sware he, that they should not enter into his rest, but to them that believed not?"

So we see that they could not enter into his rest because of unbelief. I'm compelled to go into the next verse because for all of my Christian friends out there who think

73

that the Gospel was established in *Matthew*, you need to read this.

> **Heb 4:1-2**   "Let us therefore fear, lest a promise being left us of entering into his rest, any of you should seem to come short of it. For unto us was the good news preached, as well as unto them."

Who is the "them"? It was them in the wilderness. The good news was preached to them, just as it is now being preached to us. The Gospel was preached to them in the wilderness. Is that what it says in your Bible?

> "But the word preached did not profit them,"

Well, who was the preacher? Moses was the preacher. Moshe — but what was he preaching? It was the word of YeHoVaH, the Gospel in the wilderness; the Gospel in the book of *Exodus*, the Gospel in the book of *Leviticus*, the Gospel in the books of *Numbers* and *Deuteronomy*. It's all Gospel unless the Hebrew writers got it wrong. And what was the problem?

> "...the word preached did not profit them, not being mixed with faith in them that heard it."

How do we harden our hearts today?

1. We ignore His voice

In the book of *Hosea* chapter number four — many of you know part of this verse, but let's read the whole verse.

> **Hos 4:6**   "My people are destroyed for lack of knowledge..."

That's where the Baptists stop.

"My people are destroyed for lack of knowledge..."

It's amazing how Baptists, Methodists, Presbyterians and Pentecostals want to throw that verse out there like that's the end of the verse.

"My PEOPLE are DESTROYED for lack of KNOWLEDGE!"

How many of you have heard that in your churches?

"...because thou has rejected knowledge, I will also reject you that you shall be no priests to me; seeing you have forgotten the law of our Elohim, I will also forget your children."

Generational curse — that's a generational curse. When the Father says,

"I'm going to forget your children,"

That's a generation gone. Why? Because of the curse of the Law. The curse of the Law is that if you don't obey it, you will be cursed. Now, Ignore His voice. How has He spoken? How has He spoken? We're going to get to that. How do we harden our hearts?

We ignore His voice.

You see, some of us don't start out saying,

"I'm going to ignore His voice."

It's hearing His voice and not doing what He says. That's a form of ignoring Him. I'm not going to ignore it, I'm just not going to do it. Well, you don't say:

"I'm not going to do it."

You just don't do it because other stuff gets in the way and gets ahead of what He says. Pretty soon you've forgotten it. Some people heard these messages years ago. I'm amazed some times. And again, you know, I'm not talking about people, but I hear this all the time.

> "You know, I heard this message ten years ago, and I walked away from it."

How many people that we encounter have heard about the name and who have heard about the Sabbath; and people who used to keep the Sabbath, but religion got mixed in with it? All the religion and all the traditions choked the real word out. People left the church not because of the Father, but because of the religion and the traditions and all the stuff that was added that became requirements in order to be a part of it.

So one way we harden our heart is by ignoring His voice. A second way is:

2. Refuse to listen to His voice

> "I don't care what God said."

Or,

> "I know what He said, but. I know what the Bible says, but."

I mean, think about that. Remember the times you said that? I certainly remember the times I've said it.

> "Well, I know what the word says, but."

In other words I am saying,

> "Yeah, I know that's true, but that doesn't apply here."

Why?

"Because I am exempt from the word. I've got a better way. I know what the word says, but that doesn't work. I know what the word says, but you don't know who I'm dealing with."

So in other words, He says,

"Here's what I am going to do."

I know what He says, but I'm not going to do that. I'm going to do it this way. Third:

3. Disobey His voice

And then Fourth:

4. Do not do what He tells us to do.

That's like disobeying it, but it's like — it's amazing how many people hide in church. You know, I'm going to show up. I'm going to look like everybody else. I'm going to play the role. But let me tell you that when the sun goes down, oh, I've got plans. Oh yeah, I'm going to go through the motion. I'm going to put on the good game face, the Sabbath face, the Torah face.

When we listen and walk in obedience to what YeHoVaH says, we prosper. If you look back at every time you were obedient to what He said, you would see the hand of the Almighty. We walk in the realm of life and blessings. We have peace. We feel good about ourselves. When we listen and walk in obedience to what YeHoVaH says, we are able to hear His voice more clearly for ourselves and for others.

When we don't listen and we walk in disobedience to what YeHoVaH says, we walk in the realm of death and curses. We don't have peace. We don't feel good about ourselves. There's a sense of nervousness, anxiety and fear.

When we don't listen and we walk in disobedience to what YeHoVaH says, we feel guilty. A lot of us — the guilt that we feel because of whatever is because of disobedience. It is like when we lie, we feel guilty. When we sneak, we feel guilty. When we do something we are not supposed to do, we feel guilty. Whether you know it or not, it emits signals.

Now children aren't wise enough. No, no, no, not wise. Children haven't learned how to lie with a straight face as a child. But if you are a liar and you grow up, you become a liar who can lie with a straight face and look believable even though you are lying. We have encountered a lot of them. They tell us one thing and they do something else and we believed them.

When we do stuff we know we're not supposed to do — this is why Adam and Eve — this is why Eve hid. They knew that they had done something they weren't supposed to. They felt guilty. They didn't feel good about themselves. They were ashamed of what they had done. They hide from the very person who is able to save them. People hide from God. They think:

> "I'm not going to go up in that church house and play with God. I'm not going to play with the Lord; like them hypocrites up in there. They are all up in there playing with the Lord. They know they are not living right. I am not like that!"

You have people hiding in the church and you have people hiding in the world because they think that God doesn't see them. They know what they are doing, but they think that He doesn't see them and that He can't help them. Ultimately what they are saying is that they don't want His help.

> "When I am ready for Him, THEN I'll get it
> right. When I'M ready. I'm not ready yet.
> I'm too young. I've got too much life ahead
> of me. I've got too many things I want to
> do. I can't do that if I start serving Him."

Some people are hell-bent on making a disaster of their lives. They get to the pinnacle of what it is they thought they wanted, only to jump off head-first.

**The whole duty of man is to fear Him
and to keep His commandments!**

Even if you don't know His voice, you know His word. His word and His voice are the same. And when we begin to apply the word and become committed to applying the word that He has laid out before us, then He says, Okay. Notice how long Israel was in Egypt without hearing His voice.

See how long they were in the wilderness before He decided to meet with them. You see how long He told them to get ready and prepare themselves so that He can visit with them. And you see after all of that, when they finally had an encounter with Him, what did they do?

They are no different than we are. Why? When you come into the presence of the Almighty; when you make the decision that you are going to walk with Him, what is He going to do? He is going to correct you. He is going to discipline you. He's going to admonish you. He's going to tell you things. Listen.

> "You know, I've already had enough! I've
> had enough people telling me what I can't
> do. I've had enough of people telling me
> what I should do and what I shouldn't do.

I've had enough of people trying to ruin my life or run my life, or tell me where I can go or where I can't go. I have had enough! I am living my life, MY WAY because I've had enough!"

When we get to that point where we've had enough of people, even the Father is put off to the side.

"I've had enough."

Some people would rather die than surrender.

"Here's what I think of you..."

(Makes hand gesture of gun to head and pulling trigger)

"BAM! Now they'll all suffer."

Let me tell you something folks. It's easier to surrender, although it may feel hard. You see, I know right now, there's about three people. I can sense them. They are literally thinking about taking their life. They are at the end of their rope, and I'm saying to you:

"Don't do it! Don't do it!"

"Don't do it! It's not worth it!"

"<u>Father has a plan</u>."

His plan is to prosper you, to do you good, to give you a hope and a future. It is not to harm you. People who have taken advantage of you and who have misused you have been people who have been used by the enemy for the purpose of stealing, killing and destroying. The devil knows where he is going to spend eternity, and he wants to take as many people with him as possible.

Let me tell you something folks. There are people on the planet right now that have been predestined for hell! And nothing you can say is going to change it — nothing

80

you can do is going to change it. You can preach to them until you are blue in the face and they still won't get it. That is why Yeshua says,

> "Shake the dust. Why are you wasting your time with that hard head? Why are you wasting your time with that swine? Why are you casting your pearls among swine? Shake the dust off of your feet. Woe to them! You move on!"

Many of these people are in our family, and have our biological last names. But the Father hears you. He knows where you are. He knows what you are going through and He is saying,

> "Don't quit. Don't give up. There is hope. I want you to learn My voice so that I can navigate you through all of the land mines; all of the traps, all of the snares that the enemy has set to blow you up the moment you step off of the path."

When we don't listen and we walk in disobedience to what YeHoVaH says, we feel guilty, disconnected, uninspired — that's depressed. Once depression sets in, Cymbalta (drug) can't help you. What Cymbalta will do is put a mask between you and the Almighty. It will put up a shield. It will deaden your senses, deaden your mind; put your spirit to sleep, and you become a zombie, dependent upon Cymbalta. Do you hear what I am saying?

Drugs are not what you need. What you need is the physician who prescribes the medication; and the medication is the Holy Spirit.

When we don't listen and we walk in disobedience to what YeHoVaH says, we become selfish, distrustful, destructive, angry and an instrument to be used by the devil. This is where the majority of the people walking on the planet are today.

> **Rev 3:19**   "As many as I love, I rebuke. As many as I love, I chasten: As many as I love, be zealous therefore, and repent."

What He is saying in *Revelation* is no different than what He is saying in a sense to the children of Israel. He says,

> "I brought you out. Why? Why do I want you to know Me, to hear My voice? It is because I need to correct you. I need to discipline you. I need to admonish you. I need to rebuke you. I need to chasten you so that you can repent."

> **Rev 3:20**   "Behold, I stand at the door, and knock: if any man hear my voice, and open the door, I will come in to him, and will sup with him, and he with me."

> **Rev 3:22**   "He that hath an ear, let him hear what the Spirit saith unto the congregations/assembly."

(Prayer)

Part 3 Introduction:

On Shabbat here, what we do is, I share with you what Father has given me. Unless you are one of those types of teachers that you buy your sermons on the internet, you have to get into the word for yourself.

I say that, but in denominations that I was in, the sermons would come to you via the Postmaster. They would tell you what you had to preach and especially if you are in certain seasons; you get your bulletins. You don't make up your own bulletins. Your bulletins are sent to you. Everybody is on the same page because the denomination has already sent the outline of what you are going to teach and all of that good stuff.

Then there are pastors who work and they would say they don't have time. So it is easy to go on the internet, find a sermon; even the PowerPoints of some sermons and then preach those. What I'm trying to share with you is how I research; how I study. Here is what I believe. I believe that if we've got the proper tools in which we can go and study the scripture, then we would generally (not always), but we would generally all come to the same conclusion.

Now of course when the denominations put their spin on it and all of that, then chances are we won't come to the same conclusion. But if we are using the same kinds of tools and applying the same kinds of principles, then generally we will be coming close to what the Bible actually teaches. Unfortunately too many people are dependent upon somebody else to do the work and we don't want to be like that.

What we're trying to do is to give you tools that you can use to research the scriptures for yourself and learn how to feed yourself. Halleluiah.

I already know who I am and you should know who you are. You see, we don't need somebody else to affirm who we are because we should know. This is the confidence we have in Him, you see. But the bottom line, as I've shared with you all — is that every one of us who has been called to ministry; everyone of us who claims to be the son or the daughter of the Almighty, everyone of us who claims to be born again, that means that you are called into ministry. And the key part of ministry is being available. That's key. It is being available.

There are people all over the globe who are searching for someone who represents the Almighty. The eyes of the Lord are going to and fro throughout the whole earth. This is what He says. He is looking for those whose hearts are perfect toward Him. We live in a world of people who are hurting. They are looking. They have been deceived by many. Now they are looking for that which is genuine and they sometimes just need to make a physical connection.

There are too many brothers and sisters in Messiah who want to preach, who want to have a title, who want to be recognized, but who aren't available. Do you follow what I'm saying? When people call you — if you make yourself available, you should answer the phone. I hate getting voice mail, I really do, especially when you leave a message and folks don't call you for three or four days. I'm glad I'm not dying when I'm leaving this message. Do you understand what I'm saying? We have to be available folks.

One of the responsibilities that Father had placed upon my heart was the fact that we have so many people in the body of Messiah who are not walking in the fullness of health. They have the knowledge of the Bible. They have the Torah. They may have the name, and yet their bodies are racked with pain and sickness and disease and those kinds of things.

One of the important things about what Yeshua called us and commanded us — He didn't send us out to go and have Evangelistic crusades so people can ask Jesus into their heart. Now, don't get me wrong, there's nothing wrong with that. But his commission was for us to go and make disciples. We are to make disciples for Messiah. In doing that, what happens is that this is how we as a ministry are fruitful and multiply.

It doesn't matter how many people come into this building, you see. That's not the multiplying. We should grow as a congregation. We should grow as a ministry. But what is real multiplication is the duplication of discipleship when disciples are equipped and able to do ministry. One of the things that I realized a long time ago and it just came to a head again in Dallas, is that there are way too many people for me to pray for.

There are not enough of us, brothers. We're a handful of people and we can't do it all. The Father didn't call us to do it all. We have to teach faithful individuals who will then teach faithful individuals who will then teach faithful individuals. So this is a training center. I'm not here to preach at you. I'm here to equip you. Amen?

Part 3 Teaching:

As we note from *Genesis* to *Revelation*, we know that Father is speaking. We know that. How do we learn to hear His voice? This is the key. We need to learn to hear the voice of the Almighty. The way we learn how He speaks is that we learn how He has spoken in the past. In order for you to at least discern how He speaks, is to understand how He has spoken; because He has. How does He speak today?

> **The way we learn how He speaks, is to see how He has already spoken in the past.**

We need to be asking. I'm teaching these things because here is what I have learned as a minister. People will focus on the things that we teach. They won't focus (in a congregational setting) on things that we don't teach. They focus on the things that we teach. This is why I teach on some of the things that I teach.

I teach on how to hear the voice of the Almighty so that you will focus on that. I teach on how to operate in the power of the Spirit so that you will focus on that. If I taught on Torah, that is what you will focus on — and we teach on Torah. But there is a lot more to it. We have been given the power of the Holy Spirit to manifest the works of the Almighty in the earth. Hallelujah somebody.

So how does He speak today? We need to know. Where does He speak to you? Some of you have heard when I talk about finding that place. Every last one of us in this room at some point in our lives have heard the voice of the Almighty, whether we recognized it or not.

There is the voice of the Almighty. Sometimes we don't recognize it, like Samuel. I was sharing with a sister who called me a few days ago. If you remember, Samuel was in the house of Eli, but he didn't know the voice. The voice was so real to him; he thought it was Eli speaking to him.

Many of us are like Samuel in a sense. We hear the voice of the Almighty, but because we don't recognize the voice of the Almighty, we may not necessarily respond to Him. I've heard His voice. Many of you — you've heard your name called and you looked back. How many of you have ever had that experience? You see. You hear it and you look back and because you don't see anything, you think,

> "Okay, maybe it's just my imagination playing tricks on me."

But the fact of the matter is that every last one of us, I believe has heard the voice of the Almighty. So it's a matter of learning how He speaks and then that place where we heard Him. Those of you who remember that we have been teaching and I believe if you go back to some of the Thursday Discipleship Training classes, I don't know exactly what number it was, but it is the *Evolution of Biblical Hermeneutics* part 4 and part 5.[1]

In the *Evolution of Biblical Hermeneutics,* I touched on some of this. What we recognize here is that when we begin to recognize this place where Father speaks — Abraham recognized the place where He spoke, and he built an altar. Those of you who haven't heard the teaching, we did a teaching about the altar. We did a teaching about the dedication.

On the altar, we noted that when Father spoke to certain people in the Bible, they built an altar. That was a place where they know that they heard His voice. And typically we see that when they wanted to hear His voice again — because Abraham heard His voice at times. He went other places; built an altar and nothing happened. He returned to where he had first built an altar and there he had the same encounter again. We need to recognize those places where Father speaks to us.

I've identified some places. You've heard me say several times how I ride and I don't listen to the radio. I don't listen to music. I don't have a problem with music. I don't have a problem with radio, but I'm not interested in what they have to say — especially if those are the times when the Father is revealing things to me.

There have been times when I'm driving up and down the highway and I'll always, always have something to write with and something to write on whenever I am in my vehicle. Because when Father speaks to me, I don't trust my mind. Now I remember good stuff. I remember. But I noticed something about myself. My short-term memory is not as good as my long-term memory. Do you hear what I am saying?

---

[1] See classes 23 and 24 of our Discipleship Training Program at http://discipleship101.tv

Your long-term memory is a lot longer than your short-term memory. Most of us remember the bad stuff that happened to us, even though it happened 20 or 30 years ago. For those of you who are 20, 30 years old, you remember some of that stuff as if it happened yesterday. But then when it comes down to a lot of the good that has happened, much of that stuff we don't remember. Do you hear what I'm saying? Many of you have had some wonderful experiences and you have to work hard to remember those. But you remember the bad stuff, you see.

So I write it down. There have been times that I pull over to the side of the road. If I get in my truck and I don't have the music on, I know that is a place where Father speaks to me. And then we know. Note what Yeshua said, folks. This is why I don't trust my mind. You say,

"You don't trust your mind?"

No, I don't trust myself to remember. Now I do remember, but here's what the Bible says. Yeshua said,

> "When the word of YeHoVaH has been sown in the heart, the enemy comes immediately. He comes to steal it. If he can take that word out of you before you get a chance to operate in it, you will never see the expectation that you should have; and the manifestation of why the Father spoke to you in the first place."

That's what he is coming for. He is coming for the word. He doesn't want you to have a relationship. He doesn't want you to be able to hear the Father's voice. So he creates all these other voices. You've got people talking about how instead of getting in a place where they are quiet like Habakkuk talks about (waiting and expecting the

Father to speak to them), we have a tendency to ask other people.

> "Well, what do you think God is saying to me?"

> "Well, well..."

Then we look at signs. You know signs are not where you should be looking. A wicked and adulterous generation looks for signs. Now that doesn't mean the Father doesn't speak through signs. But that is not what you should be looking for.

> "Well that didn't happen so maybe God is not...Well this didn't happen...Well maybe, you know, that door opened, so maybe that's God's will."

That's not how Father works. Father doesn't want you to be led like that. He wants you to be led by the Spirit. But you've got to get in-tune with Him and you have to recognize how He speaks.

Where does He speak? Where have you heard His voice before, and what is the last thing He said? What I've found is that way back in the earlier part of my ministry, I remember so clearly. New people who come to Messiah; even new people who come to Jesus — because I didn't know Yeshua back then, I knew Jesus. I knew Jesus in the Baptist Church. I knew Jesus in the Baptist Church that I went to because my life had fallen apart.

That Jesus — I wanted to know who God was, and you know, the son. I called on Jesus like many of us, you see. And Father began to develop a relationship with me even though I didn't know His voice at the time.

But I remember very clearly. Those of you who have heard this testimony, you know. My wife left me. She left me because I was not a good person. She filed for divorce.

It was almost two years before the divorce was finalized and Father began to deal with her and deal with me. But He started dealing with me and one of the things He said to me was,

> "I need you to tell your wife everything that you have done. You need to come clean. You need to confess."

Well, my rationale says that if my wife knows the things that I have done, how in the world am I going to get her back? That just doesn't make sense. Do you know how we rationalize? Father had to teach me that He was smarter than I was. Now some of us haven't learned that lesson yet. But He is smarter than you. He knows what's best for you even though you think you know what's best for you. He said,

> "I want you to tell your wife everything that you've ever done."

And I said,

> "Father you must be out of your mind! This is not the voice of the Almighty."

I remember distinctly as I am trying to rationalize with Him, I didn't hear that voice any more. It's like you know, the only image I had — some of you know that my favorite movie growing up was a movie called *Boy's Town, USA*. And I had the image of this Catholic Church where the priest goes into the confession booth and the confessor, the person who needs to confess, goes into the other side. The priest opens up the little window. I got this image of the Almighty. When I did not do what He said do, the window closed.

From that point on, I didn't hear His voice until I did what He told me to do. Sometimes we have to ask ourselves, what is the last thing He said — especially if we are not hearing Him, and did we do what He told us to do?

The King James Bible reads in *Hebrews* chapters 1:1-2:

> **Heb 1:1** "God, who at sundry times and in divers manners spoke in time past unto the fathers by the prophets"

He spoke to the fathers by the prophets.

> **Heb 1:2** "Hath in these last days spoken unto us by his Son, whom he hath appointed heir to all things, by whom also he made the worlds;"

In *Numbers* chapter 12 verse 6 we find:

> **Nu 12:6** "And he said, 'Hear now my words; If there be a prophet among you, I YeHoVaH will make myself known unto him in a vision, and I will speak unto him in a dream.'"

This is how Father is saying He is going to make Himself known to the prophet through a vision. He's going to make Himself known to the prophet through dreams. These are some of the ways Father speaks. What other ways has He spoken? YeHoVaH spoke at different times and in different ways to our fathers by the prophets. He spoke audibly. He spoke in actual words. There are too many people today — I hear them say,

> "You can't hear God. He doesn't speak audibly."

Well, you tell that to the people who heard Him. Even though they didn't recognize that it was Him speaking, you tell that to them and tell them what they heard was not His voice; especially after they have proven it to be His voice and it is confirmed by other people.

YeHoVaH spoke verbally to Adam and to Eve. He spoke to the serpent, right?

> "Because you have done this — on your belly."

He is talking to this animal. He spoke to Cain. In the church I grew up in, they said that you know, after Adam and Eve fell, God stopped talking. He stopped communicating. Man's relationship with the Almighty was broken. Then from that point on He only spoke to prophets and He came and went. Well, we see that even after the fall He's having a conversation with Cain, right? He speaks to Noah.

When you think about it, Noah is building an Ark and Father is out in the wilderness commanding animals to make their way to Noah's Ark. Noah didn't go and find those animals. He sent them to him. It's amazing. He only sent the number that He told Noah was going to go on the Ark. I'm sure there were a whole lot more animals on the planet than the ones that He sent to Noah.

The Father speaks to animals. Ask Balaam. He spoke to Abraham. He spoke to Isaac, to Jacob; to Moses. What I find absolutely fascinating is that He spoke to the entire company; the entire congregation of Israel, audibly. Every person that came out of Egypt to the base of that mountain heard the voice of the Almighty. That was His plan.

The Father's plan was never for Moses to be a mediator. If you look at *Exodus* chapter 19 and *Exodus* chapter 20 and you read it, you will see that while the Father is speaking to the children of Israel, Moses is right there in the midst of them.

YeHoVaH spoke audibly to the entire company. We see:

Exodus 20:18 "And all the people saw the thunderings, and the lightnings, and the noise of the trumpet, and the mountain smoking: and when the people saw it, they removed, and stood afar off."

Father had told Moses to go and to command the people to prepare themselves. You've got to understand something folks. The people of the Almighty had been in bondage (according to the prophecy He spoke to Abraham) for four hundred and thirty years. He says that they are going to be in a strange land for four hundred and thirty years. They are going to be oppressed, but woe to those people who mistreat them. And now Father sends His servant to Egypt and gathers not only the Israelites, but the multitude that decided to join themselves with Israel. They are now all at the base of the mountain.

Moses commanded them what the Father said to them. And they said,

"Okay Moses, we're going to do whatever you said that He said to do."

Now they are at the base of the mountain and the Father — you've got to understand something. Before there were ever stones written, Father spoke these commands. He introduced Himself to His people. He said,

"You all get ready because I want you to know who I am. I'm going to reveal Myself to you. I'm going to speak to you."

It was His plan to be able to speak to every last one of those individuals and to have a relationship with every last one of them. One of the things that we have to do ladies and gentlemen when we are looking at the Bible, is that we have to not just look at the surface of what is there. Every last one of those individuals had a story — every last one of them. We don't know who lost their mother in Egypt. We don't know who was raped. We don't know who was beaten to death. We know that when Moses showed up on the scene, their lives got more difficult.

Sometimes when the Savior shows up, everything is not going to be peaches and cream. When Moses shows up, Moses goes to Egypt. He goes to Pharaoh and he gives Pharaoh the instructions that the Father gave to him to give to Pharaoh. And Pharaoh says,

> "I am not hearing this. I am not trying to hear this. I don't know that God you are talking about."

He begins to take out the frustration that he is having with Moses on the very people that Moses has come to deliver. They end up being treated even more harshly. Now they have to make bricks without straw. The things that they did have were being taken away from them all because a Savior shows up.

How many times have we heard people say,

> "You know, ever since..."

I had a brother tell me just this week. He said,

> "You know, ever since I started listening to your teachings, all hell has broken loose in my life."

Well you see, the deal is that all hell had broken loose in your life, you just didn't know it! That's the bottom line. As a matter of fact, it is what is going on in people's life that drives them to want to be saved in the first place.

People whom everything is going well with — they are not looking for salvation. They are not looking for a church. They are not looking for a preacher. They are not looking for a prophet.

> "Hey — it's all good! I've got a good job. My family is doing well. I have money in the bank. We are cruising. We don't have need of anything."

Those people are not calling on the name of the Almighty unless they already have a relationship with Him. Remember Job? The devil said,

> "The reason why Job is not going to curse you and die — or the reason why Job is not going to denounce you is because you've got your protection around him. Remove your protection from around him and he will curse you to your face."

There are times when things in our lives keep us from making the commitment to the Father that we need to make. The Father has a tendency to just remove those things out of the way. I know for a fact, that is what He did to me. We make our wives our gods. We make our children our gods — we make our businesses, our jobs, our stuff. And sometimes Father has to just remove everything; just get it all out of the way. Now it is just you and Me. Now who are you going to blame?

That is because He is trying to get us to a certain place. But often times when He is calling us, we're not listening. And often times it is because we really don't want to know — don't want to adhere to what we are hearing. When the people saw this, Father revealed Himself to them.

As I was saying, those children of Israel, every last one of them had a story — every last one of them. You have to understand. These guys had been oppressed. They had been in slavery and slaves are typically not treated well. They are property like some wives are. Ouch. Verse 19:

Ex 20:19 "And they said unto Moses, 'Speak thou with us, and we will hear: but let not God speak with us, lest we die.'"

So what is this saying?

"We don't want Him to talk to us. You go talk to Him for us."

And do you know, on this day I can imagine that the Father was heartbroken even though He already knew, and I'm going to show you why.

Ex 20:20 "And Moses said unto the people, 'Fear not: for God is come to prove you, and that his fear may be before your faces, that ye sin not'"

You see, the Father wants you to know who He is so that you would understand the righteous fear you should have. He says,

"I've come to prove them."

This is what Moses is saying.

"Don't be afraid of Him!"

Moses knew this because Moses had already had a chance to know Him. Not only had Moses had a chance to know Him, it was the Father who had initiated the conversation with Moses. It was the Father who had initiated the relationship with Moses. It is the Father who initiates the relationship with us. Why? Because He wants you to know Him. He wants us to know Him. He wants us to know Him more than we might want to know Him. Why? Because He has plans. He has a plan for every last one of you.

Once we know the plan that He has, then we get vision. Without vision people cast off restraints. If you don't know where you are supposed to be going, you are liable to go anywhere. If you don't know who you are supposed to be with, you are liable to be with anybody.

You have to know the people that the Father wants you to be connected to. It is in the connections that the Father has which get you to the right place. How do you think the Father orders the steps of the righteous? Well, first the righteous have to be righteous. Now how do you act righteous? You seek first the Kingdom of YeHoVaH and His righteousness.

Well, how do you do that? You get into His word. You see, the word made flesh is the Father who was in the beginning. When you get in His word, you are literally getting to know Him. A reading of the Bible is like a conversation with the Almighty if your heart is open for Him to speak to you through His word. He wants you to know Him.

Notice what He says. He has come to prove you. Now notice this. The word here is "*nacah*" (naw-saw), which is a primitive root. It means actually, to test. That is literally what it means. He has come to test you. Now He doesn't come to tempt us, because James says that He doesn't tempt anybody. But He tests us. Now you get the word tempt from here. But He comes to test.

This is the second time YeHoVaH proves or tests the people. Remember the first time is in *Exodus* chapter 16:4. In *Exodus* chapter 16, the people are crying out and they are hungry and the Father says,

> "You know, I'm going to give them some manna."

Exodus 16:4 says:

> **Ex 16:4** "Then said YeHoVaH unto Moses, 'Behold, I will rain bread from heaven for you; and the people shall go out

and gather a certain rate every day, that I
may prove them,'"

Why is He proving them with manna? He is trying to get them to understand the importance of what is coming next. You see, He proves them with the Sabbath. He proves them with the Sabbath. This is what He does. He says,

"Six days I am going to rain manna. On the
seventh day there is not going to be any
manna — don't go looking for it."

But there were some folks who went out and looked for it anyway and He got angry. If you read the rest of *Exodus* chapter 16, you will see. But let's read this. He says:

"I will rain bread from heaven for you; and
the people shall go out and gather a certain
rate every day, that I may prove them,
whether they will walk in My law, or no."

You see, He doesn't give the Law until *Exodus* chapter 20. But here He is in *Exodus* chapter 16, and he is testing them. He is testing them with the manna before He gives them the Law. But when He gives them the Law, they don't want to hear it because He has already tested them in the Sabbath. So the Father is not surprised when the people decide they don't want to have this relationship with Him because He has already tested them.

The first time YeHoVaH tests the people, it is through the instructions given to Moses concerning the manna and the Sabbath. He tests them with the Sabbath to see if they would keep the Law. He comes to speak to them, whereas before He spoke to them through Moses.

"Moses, now I want you to give the people the instructions. This is what I want them to do."

"Okay."

He tests them with the verbal instruction from His servant before He actually speaks to them. Do you see this? He tests them with the verbal instruction through His servant Moses before He actually speaks to them audibly. But based on their response to His servant Moses, they have already proven that they don't want that kind of relationship with Him.

The second time YeHoVaH tests the people is through His own voice.

"I'm going to give you the Sabbath. If you keep the Sabbath, you will keep the rest of my commandments. I'm going to show you what is in your heart. I'm going to test you with the Sabbath because if you don't keep the Sabbath, you are not going to keep the rest of the commands."

As a matter of fact when He gets upset with them, He says,

"How long do I have to put up with you guys? Why do you violate My commandments?"

He hasn't given them yet — *Exodus* 16, *Exodus* 20. So now He comes. He doesn't get to commandment number eleven. If you read it in *Exodus*, you see. He speaks. By the time He gets to the tenth command, the people are saying,

"You know what? I can't take any more. No more. We don't want Him talking to us."

Imagine. We don't know, but imagine had they not done that. Is it possible that Father would have continued to give them the instructions that He gave to Moses right there at the foot of the mountain? You see, He did not stop speaking to them. They stopped wanting to hear, and that is the problem that we face today folks. You say,

"Well, I DO want to hear His voice."

Do you really? I mean, do you really? Because I want you to — if you really want to hear His voice, how much time do you set aside expecting Him to speak to you? How long are you willing to sit in silence? Do you really? How much time do you have for Him? How much time do you spend in prayer? Do you spend all the time talking?

"Okay, thank you Father, Amen, see ya!"

Do you *really* want to hear Him? Because just as He is getting ready to speak you know, we have our hour in. We are folding up our tallit, you see. And Father is saying,

"Where are you going?"

How much time do we set aside? This is where Habakkuk comes in. He says,

"Listen. I've got my paper. I've got my pencil. I know He is going to speak. So I'm going to sit here and I'm going to wait until He does."

You've got to have that kind of tenacity. Father says,

"Do you really want to hear Me? Do you really? Take the time. Seek Me. I'm here."

But we are so busy in life with so much to do. We've got our families. We've got our spouses. We've got our significant others. We've got our children. We've got our business. We've got our jobs. We've got our ministries. We've got all this stuff going on, and Father is saying,

> "You know, you are too busy doing ministry for Me instead of doing the ministry I want you to do."

You see folks, I don't think there is anybody in this room busier than I am. Now you may be. You may be extremely busy. But notice when I call you, do I get an answer? But when you call me, you see? How many of you have ever called me and didn't get an answer or a response the same day? Just how available are you? Our availability to our Father is going to be determined by our availability to one another. Ouch.

> **Ex 20:21**   "And the people stood afar off, and Moses drew near unto the thick darkness where God was."

> **Ex 20:22**   "And YeHoVaH said unto Moses, 'Thus thou shalt say unto the children of Israel, Ye have seen that I have talked with you from heaven.'"

Now Moses is saying,

> "Listen. I want you to…"

(YeHoVaH says:)

> "Talk to the people, and you tell them."

(Moses says:)

> "Now listen Israel, Hey, pay attention! Now all of you heard the Father speak to you from heaven, right? All of you heard it."

This is what He is saying. He says,

> "Talk to the children of Israel and tell them
> you have seen that I have talked with you."

Isn't that what He says? Father desires for His people to hear His voice. He uses tests to get us to a place of obedience so that when He speaks, our response is to obey. We hear and we obey (Shema). We are not hearers only. We hear and we obey.

1. Spoken Words

The voice of YeHoVaH speaks audibly in actual words. That is one way He speaks.

2. YeHoVaH communicates through the angel of YeHoVaH.

Now you know, it's fascinating. Well, let me not get ahead. First, communications to Moses:

> **Ex 3:2** "There the angel of YeHoVaH appeared to him in flames of fire from within a bush. Moses saw that though the bush was on fire, it did not burn up."

Moses is down in the valley. He sees this bush. He makes his way up there and the angel of YeHoVaH appears to him. Now, what is fascinating is how even after the Holy Spirit is given on the day of Shavuot in *Acts* chapter 2, the angel of YeHoVaH is still active throughout the book of *Acts*. Do you see this? The angel of YeHoVaH spoke to the Apostles. Now these men are filled with the Spirit.

> **Ac 5:19-20** "But the angel of YeHoVaH by night opened the prison doors, and brought them forth, and said, 'Go, stand and speak in the temple to the people all the words of this life.'"

Ac 8:26 "And the angel of YeHoVaH spoke unto Philip, saying, 'Arise, and go toward the south unto the way that goeth down from Jerusalem unto Gaza, which is desert.'"

He meets the Ethiopian eunuch there. *Acts* chapter 12, verse 7, the angel of the Lord appears.

Ac 12:7 "And, behold, the angel of YeHoVaH came upon him, and a light shined in the prison: and he smote Peter on the side, and raised him up, saying, 'Arise up quickly.' And his chains fell off from his hands."

Ac 12:8 "And the angel said unto him, 'Gird thyself, and bind on thy sandals.' And so he did. And he saith unto him, 'Cast thy garment about thee, and follow me.'"

And the angel went.

Ac 12:9 "And he went out, and followed him; and wist not that it was true which was done by the angel; but thought he saw a vision."

See, here he's having an encounter with an angel, but in his mind he thinks he is seeing a vision. Now it is interesting what *Hebrews* says.

Heb 13:2 "Be not forgetful to entertain strangers: for thereby some have entertained angels unawares."

It is amazing how people have shown up in my life at times. I have no idea who these people are. There have been times when we've needed something and someone shows up out of the wild blue yonder (as they would say). They meet the need and they are gone; never to be heard from again. I don't try to figure this stuff out, but I try to recognize it.

"Well, maybe that was an angel."

In the non-profit arena, they have terms for people who are in fundraising. There are terms for big donors. Big donors in non-profit arenas are considered to be angels. That is what they call them. Anybody in non-profit? Anybody ever been in a non-profit? Anybody ever heard the term that a donor is associated as an angel? We've got angels in this ministry. Whenever there is a need, they come through.

The Father knows your need. And what I have found out about the Father is that the lower my need is, the lower my expectation of Him. This is one of the things you have taught me, Michael. You don't know you have taught me this, but you have taught me this.

You have taught me so many things. I watch you and how you operate in your ministry, and I know you worry. But you don't look like you worry. That is because you expect Father to do what you are believing Him to do. We have to expect. We have to have expectation. If you don't have expectation, then don't expect. If you don't expect something from Him, you are not going to get it.

When we are operating in what He has called us to do, how in the world can the Father call us to do something and not give us the resources to do it? Now this is not arrogance, but I have a right to expect Him to meet the needs if He has called me to do something. He is not going to call me to work and then I have to figure out where I am going to get the tools to do the work. Do you hear what I am saying?

Is He going to call you into the service and then not provide the needs for you to get the job done? I don't think

He does that. As a matter of fact, from what I read in the Bible, there is not one example that I see. As a matter of fact, Father knows exactly what you need. He knows exactly where it is at.

I remember in Michigan, Father began to talk to us about coming here. And you know on the surface, everything looked like it was fine for us. People don't know that when you are the head of a ministry and you have employees and you have utilities and you have rent, you have all of these people. They are not coming to the secretary for their money. The phone company is looking to the people who signed the contract. The bank is looking for the folks who — where does the buck stop in this organization? That is what they are looking for. Everybody else is doing their thing.

The burden of the work is upon the person who is responsible for making sure that all of those soldiers have what they need to get the jobs that they have gone into the organization to do. I mean, it is not even right for the job to hire you.

> "We're going to hire you. We want you to work on this imaginary machine, but we want you to produce real parts."

It doesn't work. They bring you in. They give you the job. They give you what you need; the resources to make it happen. And if you don't have the resources, you make that known. They are responsible to make sure you get those resources if they expect you to do your job effectively and efficiently, you see. It is the same thing with the Father. As the head of an organization, the one who is in the office with the door closed crying out to YeHoVaH because you don't know if you are going to make payroll this week — folks I'm telling you.

I'm up in Michigan and we were making things happen. I can't tell you how many times I had to meet the gas guy at the door before he turned it off to write him a check. I had to keep watch for the water guy because if the truck pulled up and he got out with this long tool, I knew that he's about to turn something off. I have to go out there and make sure that he gets paid so he can go on about his business. Anybody run ministry business? You know what I'm talking about.

Father is going to make sure you have what you need. It's a matter of managing those needs. But here we are in Michigan and Father says,

> "Okay, I want you to go to North Carolina, and I want you to establish ministry in Charlotte; not knowing anybody. I want you to leave all of that stuff."

I will never forget. I was in Dallas again for Hanukkah — Plano, and come to find out here we are in Charlotte, living here. It's a seventeen-thousand square foot building in Michigan in the middle of winter with a flat roof, and all of this snow and ice built up on the roof. The roof and the ceiling started to collapse. The snow melts and goes down all of the walls and all of the plaster. It literally destroyed this facility that we'd left in Michigan to come here.

Now I have to tell you. Chances are, had we been there, that might not have happened, but we don't know. I don't know. But I know that it created a hardship for us because we've got a facility that we need to off-load and now the condition of it is a lot worse than it was in its prime.

But the Father said,

> "Don't worry about that stuff. This is where you are to be."

106

And you see, I have learned that voice. When He says "Go," you need to move. At least that is the way that it has been for me. So here we are doing ministry. The next thing I know, Father says,

> "I want you to tell Michael: 'Michael, I believe you are supposed to bring your studio to Charlotte.'"

And lo and behold, here he is. There are other people that I have spoken to.

Folks, let me tell you something. The voice of the Almighty is so important for us to learn. And therefore we know that Father will speak to us. He will even visit with you. One of the words that they use in theological circles is *Theophany*. It is a visible appearance of God, generally in human form — an angel of YeHoVaH or however He decides to show up. I remember times when I'm trying to soak out His voice. There are times in my life when I have literally tried to shut the voice of YeHoVaH off because I didn't want to hear Him.

Can we be honest up in here? I am sitting in a bar drinking Johnny Walker Red, and the more I drank, the more sober I got. It doesn't make sense. I can't even get drunk up in here. And I remember this drunken guy sitting next to me saying,

> "What are you doing in here? You don't belong up in here."

> "What?"

The drunk next to me is telling me I don't belong in the bar, and I didn't. But the point is, this is what I have recognized. There are many people out there who are trying to bury their head in a bottle, in a drug; in some form of what do you call it, intoxicant. I believe that most addicts out there have the hand of YeHoVaH on their life. Most people who are alcoholics out there have the hand of the Almighty on their life.

Because of circumstances and things that have happened to them, they are trying to drown their sorrow in a bottle. But no matter how much they drink, no matter how much they get high, no matter how much they use, they can't get away from the voice in their head. The hard part of this ladies and gentlemen is that the day is going to come when we have to sober up. You see, I found out that for me, that one of the reasons why I continued to drink was because I didn't want to be sober.

The reason why I didn't want to be sober is because I had to deal with reality. I had to deal with the messes I made. I had to deal with the people I had wronged. I've had to deal with the fact that I am responsible for why my wife left me. I had to deal with a whole lot of things in my life that I didn't want to deal with. And that sober reality is so painful that we drink and get high to avoid it. You have to go through the pain. You've got to sober up. You've got to be sober-minded.

3. YeHoVaH communicated through dreams.

4. YeHoVaH communicated through visions; and to believers and to unbelievers.

Check out these next things. He communicated to Abimelech. Look at this.

> **Ge 20:3**   "But God came to Abimelech in a dream by night, and said to him, 'Behold, thou art but a dead man,'"

That's what He said!

> "I'm going to kill you. You mess with this man's wife..."

Now notice this conversation because I find the conversation to be absolutely fascinating. He says:

> "...for the woman which thou hast taken; for she is a man's wife.'"

> **Ge 20:4** "But Abimelech had not come near her: and he said, 'Lord, wilt thou slay also a righteous nation?'"

> **Ge 20:5** "Said he not unto me, 'She is my sister?' and she, even she herself said, 'He is my brother:'"

See, often times we hear this story and we say that Abraham lied. But I think that Sarah was in on it too.

> "...in the integrity of my heart and innocency of my hands have I done this."

I meant no harm in doing this. He said.

> "She's my sister."

And she said,

> "He's my brother."

And then he says:

> **Ge 20:6** "And God said unto him in a dream,"

Now Abimelech is having a conversation with the Almighty. He says,

> "Yea, I know that thou didst this in the integrity of thy heart; for I also withheld thee from sinning against me: therefore suffered I thee not to touch her."

Ge 20:7 "Now therefore restore the man his wife; for he [Hebrew: navi] is a prophet, and he shall pray for thee,"

I'm going to tell you something folks. This is just mind-boggling. Abraham goes into this community. He tells the man,

"This is my sister."

Sarah says,

"This is my brother."

He's got Abraham's wife up in his bed chamber. Abraham is down there worried about it because of his own doing. And YeHoVaH says,

"This man is my prophet. Now, I know what he has done."

He says,

"I know, I know, I know. I KNOW. So I am here to protect you. I am here to keep you from having Me kill you. So give him his wife back. I know you have some issues. He is going to pray for you."

You ought to read that story.

"...and if thou restore her not, know for sure, you WILL die, and everything that belongs to you. I am going to kill everything!"

That is my translation. YeHoVaH communicated to Pilate — to his wife in a dream. Who communicated to Pilate? Look at what she says.

> **Mt 27:19** "When he was set down on the judgment seat, his wife sent unto him, saying, 'Have thou nothing to do with that just man: for I have suffered many things this day in a dream because of him.'"

Father is up — now He probably couldn't talk to Pilot, so He is visiting Pilate's wife knowing that Pilate listens to his wife. And He now says,

> "Miss Pilate? You need to talk to your husband."

I mean this is what is happening folks — and she does.

> **Nu 12:6** "And he said, 'Hear now my words: [YeHoVaH] If there be a prophet among you, I YeHoVaH will make Myself known unto him in a vision, and will speak unto him in a dream.'"

So He speaks in dreams and visions.

> **Joel 2:28** "And it shall come to pass afterward, that I will pour out my spirit upon all flesh; and your sons and your daughters shall prophesy, your old men shall dream dreams, your young men shall see visions:"

See, Father is in this just as on Sinai. When He showed up with the children of Israel in attendance, every Israelite heard His voice. He says,

> "When I release My Spirit, every one of you — sons, daughters, old, young, male servants, female servants, everybody is going to hear Me."

That's a precious promise.

6. YeHoVaH communicates to His people through the written word.

> **Ex 17:14** "And YeHoVaH said unto Moses, 'Write this for a memorial in a book, and rehearse it in the ears of Joshua: for I will utterly put out the remembrance of Amalek from under heaven."

> **Ex 31:18** "And he gave unto Moses, when he had made an end of communing with him upon mount Sinai, two tables of testimony, tables of stone, written with the finger of God."

This is a good idea of what this may have looked like. (Shows commandments etched into a granite stone slab.) The tablets of stone that the Almighty gave to Moshe — the written word, and this is how He gave it to them. Now they probably didn't look exactly like this, but Moses came down from the mountain with these tablets.

Before He gave Moses these tablets, you've got to understand something. The only reason why these words are on a stone is because the people refused to hear the audible voice of the Almighty. That is the only reason why they are on stones.

I believe that the stones are significant to the heart of stone. Father wants to remove the stones so that He can speak to us; so that He can communicate His commandments to us. He says,

> "I'm going to make a New — A Renewed Covenant. It won't be like the old where I wrote it on tablets of stone. But this is going to be written on your heart. Everyone one

112

of you is going to know Me. No longer will a man need to say to his neighbor: 'Know YeHoVaH!' Because all are going to know Me."

That was His intent way back then. Ladies and gentlemen, I have to tell you this because the Bible says that if a prophet tries to — the way you will know a real prophet from a false prophet is that if one of you who is a prophet tries to lead people by saying to worship other gods, what should happen to him? Now when we think about the commands and what Father gave, He says:

"If anyone tries to lead you away from My word, know that that is a false teacher."

(Holds up a stone slab.)

"That is a false prophet."

Do you hear what I am saying? Now let me bring this real close to home. As a matter of fact, I am going to drive it on up into your own garage and shut the garage and leave the engine running. Any, any, ANY minister who will tell YeHoVaH's people that they don't have to keep His commands is leading them away from Him. They are not leading them to Him. They are leading them away from Him. Imagine the idea that you can have a relationship with the Almighty but you don't have to do what He says. Yeah, I said it and I am not taking it back! There are too many talking heads out there who are saying,

"We're not under the law. The law has been done away with. All you need is the blood of Jesus."

That's a part of it. Yeshua came to reconcile us to the Father. The Son did not come to deliver us from the Father, but to reconcile us to the Father. Imagine the Son saying,

"Listen. You can come in, but you don't have to keep My Father's commands. All you have to do is love."

"Well, how is that?"

You see, He said,

"If you love Me, you will keep My commands."

"Yeah, but that's in the Gospel...that's not what He meant."

Well, the writer of that passage in John — we believe wrote the first and second and third John who said that.

"If you say you love God; and you don't keep His commandments, you are a liar and the truth is not in you."

The Bible says in the book of *Revelation* that outside, those who don't have access to the trees; to the leaves of the trees that heal the nations — those who are outside are the sorcerers and whoremongers and adulterers and those who make lies. So anybody that says to us — who claims to represent the Father, who claims to be a prophet of God, who says you don't have to keep His commands, is a false prophet.

7. YeHoVaH communicates to His people by His Spirit.

I'm about to turn the corner here again.

Joel 2:28 "And it shall come to pass afterward, that I will pour out my Spirit upon all flesh; and your sons and your daughters shall prophesy, your old men shall dream dreams, your young men shall see visions:"

Ac 1:8   "But ye shall receive power,"

This is what Yeshua says, *Acts* chapter one verse eight:

> "You shall receive *dunamis*. You shall receive dynamic power. You shall receive miraculous power when the Holy Spirit is come upon you."

Martyrs — you are now going to lay down your life. You are going to pick up your own stake. You are going to be My ambassador; My mouthpiece. You are going to represent Me — not your denomination, not your pastor, not your theology. You are going to represent the Kingdom.

> "...unto me both in Jerusalem, and in all Judaea, and in Samaria, and unto the uttermost parts of the earth."

> **1 Co 2:9**   "But as it is written, Eye hath not seen, nor ear heard, neither have entered into the heart of man, the things which YeHoVaH hath prepared for them that love him."

> **1 Co 2:10**   "But YeHoVaH hath revealed them unto us by his Spirit:"

We are about to get into the work of the Holy Spirit. I wanted to get to this point so that next week I can really lock this in. We are going to identify and you're going to identify. I am going to help you identify what the Father's voice sounds like — and more particularly, how He has spoken to you. But he says:

> "...for the Spirit searcheth all things, yea, the deep things of God."

1 Co 2:11 "For what man knoweth the things of a man, save the spirit of man which is in him? Even so the things of God knoweth no man, but the Spirit of God."

We have received not the spirit of the world, but the Spirit which is of God so that we might know the things which are freely given to us by Him or of Him.

1 Co 2:13 "Which things also we speak, not in the words which man's wisdom teacheth, but which the Holy Ghost teacheth; comparing spiritual things with spiritual."

1 Co 2:14 "But the natural man receiveth not the things of the Spirit of God: for they are foolishness unto him: neither can he know them, because they are spiritually discerned."

1 Co 2:15 "But he that is spiritual judgeth all things, yet he himself is judged of no man.

1 Co 2:16 "For who hath known the mind of the Lord, that he may instruct him? But we have the mind of Messiah."

Now it is a matter of operating in that, but the challenge is that we are surrounded by the world. It is very difficult for us to be in the world and to be surrounded by the world and not take on a world philosophy because of whom we have chosen to be around.

Let me tell you something, folks. It takes a lot for you to make the decision. First of all, you have to make the decision that you are going to get to know Him. And then you've got to MAKE the decision that you are no longer going to be worldly-minded. Then you have to make the decision that you are going to seek Him and get to know His voice. You see, there is a lot that you are going to have to do in order to get to the place where you say,

"I want to know Him like that."

Our actions are what tell us who we are. Your actions tell me who you are. My actions tell you who I am. Your actions should tell you who you are. I don't need to look outside of myself to know the wretched man that I am. All I have to do is to be honest with myself.

I am brutally honest with myself because I know my thoughts even though you don't have a clue. I know what goes on in my head. I know what is going on in my heart. I know how I feel about you. I know how I feel about my wife. I know how I feel about my children. I know how I feel about the Father. I know how I feel about everything. Unfortunately we are not honest with other people; which causes us to lie to ourselves. The Bible says,

"Speak the truth and lie not."

Do not lie to one another. But many people can't handle the truth.

"Oh, yeah, I can handle the truth. I can handle the truth. Tell me, tell me."

You tell them and the next thing you know, they don't want to talk to you any more. You have to tip-toe. You have to water stuff down. You have to spoon-feed them with a long-handled spoon lest they bite your hand. I am glad Father made me a big Black man, because I can talk and folks get intimidated. I guarantee folks are a lot less likely to walk up on me than they are on you Jim (to audience member). Do you hear what I am saying?

Now understand that for me it is an advantage and I recognize that. A fellow is going to think twice about walking up on me. I won't harm anybody. Do you hear what I'm saying? But people should recognize the Spirit that is on you. The fear of — even though Israel were some scared people, the fear of YeHoVaH was shed abroad and went before them. When you walk in the light and you walk in the power and the authority of the Almighty, it is the fear of the Almighty.

I remember several times folks, listen. I've got prophecies that go way back. Most of the prophecies that I have ever received — to me the word of YeHoVaH is precious. I am telling you. I've got pages and pages. People back where I come from used to record every prophecy. Then we'd get a tape. How many of you have come out of churches like that where they speak; they prophesy and they give you a tape?

Every tape I've received; every last one of them, I went home and transcribed. Why? Because to me if this is the word of YeHoVaH, I'm going to see. One of the ways you know if a prophet is a prophet is if what they say comes to pass. Well, how do you know? One of the things that I have found in many of these prophetic ministries is that people are so in-tuned with getting a word of prophecy that they don't remember it. They get it, they get excited and they fall out under the power.

"Did you hear that word the Lord gave me?"

"Yeah, did you hear it?"

Where is it at now? Did it happen? You see, a lot of these jack-legged prophets bank on the fact that your memory is short-term. They prophesy to you this year. You get in the $500 line. You get in the $1,000 line — the $5,000 line. They give you a word for your whole family. Nothing comes to pass. They come back next week with the same old line with a different strategy. You see, when the word is sown ladies and gentlemen, you have to take that word and you have to take it and you have to guard it and hide it and watch over it. Because I didn't trust my mind, I took those tapes.

Have you ever heard — notice that they don't sell cassette tape players any more. It is hard to find one. You have to go to Goodwill or some place to find one. You can't find one in any of the stores. And you know, some of those things, you put your tape in there and it eats it right up. I didn't trust them. I wrote them down. There are some things as I go through here that haven't come to pass. But right now I am walking in the fullness of several of the things that are in these pages. Do you hear what I am saying?

You have to guard the word. The enemy is coming. He is coming. The reason why there is warfare in some of your lives is because of the word that is circling around you.

1 Ti 4:1 "Now the Spirit speaketh expressly, that in the latter times some shall depart from the faith, giving heed to seducing spirits, and doctrines of devils;"

How do you know?

Heb 3:7 "Wherefore (as the Holy Ghost saith, 'Today if ye will hear his voice,'"

Heb 3:8 "Harden not your hearts, as in the provocation, in the day of temptation in the wilderness:"

Heb 3:9 "When your fathers tempted me, proved me, and saw my works forty years."

That is the other thing. Remember the first time the Father says that He is coming to prove Israel was during the manna. The second time He comes to prove them was at Mt. Sinai. Moses says,

> "He is just trying to prove you so that you will fear Him."

Then the third time we see in *Deuteronomy* chapter 8 where Moses is recapping. He says,

> "He took you through the wilderness for forty years to prove you!"

They didn't get it with the manna. They didn't get it at Sinai. Forty years in the wilderness — and those forty years; every person who came out of Egypt, what happened to them? Their carcasses fell in the wilderness. You see, if the Father doesn't get through to you, you will wander through life never hearing His voice or obeying what He is commanding you to do. So I am hoping that through this teaching, that you will desire — and I know that it has already happened (that you have said this).

> "I want to know His voice. I want to know what He sounds like. I want to know how He sounds. I want to know how He speaks to me. I want to find that place where He speaks to me. And when I find that place where He speaks to me, I want to spend as much time in that place as I possibly can."

It is in that place that the Father reveals the plans that He has for you. He reveals the purpose for you. He shows you the connections that you are supposed to make. He shows you. I mean, as a child, I am seeing myself do things that are literally frightening me. I'm seeing myself just — what was it? Thursday. I'm walking out of this office on the other side of this wall having a conversation with Lee Eagan that I had some time in the past. And I'm standing right there at that door saying,

"Wow!"

The world might call it Déjà vu. But I believe that the Father, who knows the end from the beginning, finishes the plan before He starts it. And I believe that in our life when we come to this earth; I believe that the Father places within us. His divine plan for us and He gives us glimpses of that. And there are times in our lives when we are at certain places; or we say something, or we are with somebody and something flashes that says,

"Man, I have been here before. This is too real."

And when those things happen to me, Father is saying,

"You are right on the path."

I remember the conversations. I am remembering what we are talking about. And I know what He wants me to say and how to deal with this. What is happening? It can be scary unless you come to recognize it and to expect it. The presence of the Father will scare you just like He scared the children of Israel.

"We don't want to hear this."

You know, when He shows up folks — when He shows up, one of the responses is fear. And fear — if we don't understand what is going on, will cause us to draw back instead of embrace. The Father wants us to fear Him, but not the kind of fear that causes us to run away from Him; the kind of fear that causes us to run to Him. The righteous run to Him.

We run to Him. We don't run from Him. We don't hide ourselves. The people who don't do right are the ones who hide. They are the ones who run. He wants us to draw. He says,

> "If you draw near to Me, I will draw near to you. If you come near Me, I will come near you."

But He put the responsibility on us.

> "Do you want to know Me? Seek Me. Seek Me. As a matter of fact, seek Me first."

You are seeking a wife. You are seeking a career. You're seeking a ministry. You are seeking a future.

> "Your future is in Me. I know the plan. You don't know the plan, but I want to reveal the plan to you. But in order for Me to reveal the plan to you, you're going to have to seek Me. I have to be comfortable and confident enough that if I reveal My plan to you, are you going to do it? Are you going to obey what I am commanding you? Or are you going to be like Adam and Eve in the garden and do that which I command you not to do? Because now I who am supposed to be working with you — you have put Me in a position where I have to work against you."

I was sharing with my wife the other day. I know that as I am dealing with my children and dealing with things in life — one of the things that always brings me comfort when I have to deal hard — you know sometimes as parents, we have to lay out the cold, hard truth. Sometimes we have to deal with our children in hard ways. In the Torah, Father says, Listen. If you have a son who is disrespectful and he doesn't want to hear; he doesn't want to listen. He doesn't want to respect anyone and doesn't want to do what is required of him, what do you do with him? You take him to the elders at the city gate. Imagine a father taking his son to the elders at the city gate knowing that what waits at the city gate is the death penalty. That is a hard thing for any father to do. But this is what Father said. He said,

> "Listen. Let me show you something. Let me show you my heart, because I LOVE Adam. I LOVE the man and the woman that I made. I made a special place for them to dwell. I made everything that they needed available. They only had one command — just one. Of all of the trees in the garden, I have given them to freely eat; but they decided that they wanted to eat from the one I told them not to, and now I have to put them out."

Imagine. The Father has to put His creation out of the place that He prepared for them. And in His mercy so they didn't freeze to death or whatever, He made a coat of skin. He sacrificed an animal; showed grace, mercy. And then ultimately because He loves us so much, He put His only begotten Son through something that no other human being on the planet has ever had to deal with. That is when an innocent man is taking on the sin of the entire world. And He says,

> "This is My Son. This is MY Son."

And yet it pleased Him to put him through that. Why? Because you see, He knows the outcome. This is the thing that helps me to trust Him. Although I can't see it, He knows the outcome. He knows the outcome. Even though Yeshua — the Bible says:

"The joy that was set before him..."

He endured the cross even though the joy that was set before him caused him to endure the cross. It didn't stop him agonizing in the garden to get to it.

Folks, this is serious and the Father is trying to communicate His heart.

> "Listen. I WANT you to know Me. I WANT you to know My voice. I've got great things that I want to do for you and through you. There is a world that needs to hear what I am putting in you. But you have to be willing to allow Me to use you and to take you where I need you to go. You have to be willing to allow Me to use you. You have to be willing to lay your life down. You've got to be willing to go. You've got to be willing to leave stuff. All you can see is what you are leaving. But I see what I have in store. What I've got in store — where I am taking you is much greater than what you are leaving behind. But you will never know unless you go."

The Father is trying to bring us to that light — that plan as Jeremiah says. He knows the plan that He has for us; plans to give us a hope and a future. His plan is not to kill us. It is not to destroy us. Father has a good plan for you, ladies and gentlemen.

> **Heb 3:11**   "So I sware in my wrath, They shall not enter into my rest.)"

> **Heb 3:12**   "Take heed, brethren, lest there be in any of you an evil heart of

unbelief, in departing from the living Elohim."

In the last chapter of the book of *Acts,* the book of *Acts* closes with:

> "...and Paul dwelt two whole years in his own hired house, and received all that came in unto him, preaching the Kingdom of Elohim; and teaching those things which concerned the Master Yeshua the Messiah with all confidence, no man forbidding him."

This is how *Acts* ends, but this is really not an end of a book. You see, the book of *Acts* is still being written. For those who want to say that the Bible is complete, it really is not. Today, right now, tomorrow, next week, every last one of us has a place in this book — every last one of you. It's not over. It's not over until He says that it is over, you see. I just want you all to be encouraged.

Part 4 Teaching:

I want to say a few things before we go further, because I really believe that people need to know. I need to tell you that it was never my desire to do what I am doing. I did not want to preach. I didn't want to be a teacher in a church.

I remember several years ago, my wife — she must have said this at least fifteen times over the course of our marriage — that she did not marry a preacher.

I think there were times when she felt as if she had been tricked. I certainly felt there were times when I have been tricked. I just want to be honest with you. I think that there've been times when Father has used situations to maneuver me into a position that I really didn't want to be in.

My choice was to run. My choice was to choose the path that I wanted. For those of you who don't know, I have a degree in culinary arts. For several years in the military, I was a chef. I went to school through the G.I. bill and got my degree. I did internship in the premier hotel in the city where I lived.

How many of you have ever heard of *Amway*? There is a place called the "Amway Grand Plaza" which was built by the DeVos and Van Andel families in Grand Rapids, Michigan. At the top floor of this tower was a restaurant called *Cygnus.* In this restaurant, you had to make reservations months in advance just to get in. That is where I did my internship. I saw opportunity to become this great chef. I probably would have ended up on one of those — who knows? I could have probably been on *Hell's Kitchen* (TV program) or something.

That was not the path. And during the time of meeting my wife, I was not in church getting married. I didn't want anything to do with God. But over the course of our marriage and all of the circumstances that took place, I felt as if God cornered me.

Anybody ever felt cornered? I felt cornered. I had gone through enough stuff in my life to the point where I was tired. I was tired of running. I didn't realize that a lot of us try to hide in plain sight. We don't go into the mountains or into the woods, but we put on these faces. We put on airs. We have a way that we want people to see us.

There are many times, that as an adult I would look at grown people and I would see little boys trying to be men — little boys in grown up bodies trying to sound like important men. Little girls in grown up bodies were trying to impress people with their grownness and their degrees and their positions and their homes and their cars and all of the stuff that says to the people outside of them that I am doing really, really well. Many people that I knew lived in big fancy homes and drove big fancy cars, but their marriage was in trouble.

Millionaires and "thousandaires" — folks who had all of the outward appearance of having it all together, and their lives were a wreck. Now we didn't live like that, but I am one of those stories. I knew people who couldn't buy their way out of marital problems. They spent lots of money per hour having people counsel them with various counseling methods. I am saying this to you to say that I am here doing what I am doing because I came to a place of surrender; of feeling like I didn't have a choice. I either do this or God is going to kill me. That's how I felt.

From that point on, my feelings and my emotions and my desires and my ambitions just went away. I really didn't care any more. Now I have to say that the human side of me cares very much what people think. The Spirit side of me could care less. I find myself in places like I am at right now, where I am proclaiming the word of YeHoVaH and saying things out of my mouth by the Spirit that my brain is saying,

> "You have messed up really, really bad now.
> You shouldn't have said that. You shouldn't
> have done that."

You see. I remember several times that as I was preaching in Michigan, my mother came up and visited. And while my mother was sitting in the audience, it was as if the Father put this veil over my face. Although I saw everybody there, I didn't see anybody. I'm saying things concerning my mother that were embarrassing. There have been times when I have preached and my wife is sitting in the audience. I am using illustrations of things that I did as a man married to this woman that would hurt any wife to find that their husband is proclaiming in a public setting, the unfaithfulness that he had experienced — the things that he had done while she is sitting there.

I know and knew at the time that by explaining and expressing these things, that wounds that she was working on being healed from were opened all over again. Her mother could not stand it and her mother loves me. But it was very difficult for her mother to sit in our congregation with me being as transparent about my life and about my past as I was being.

I am saying these things to you because I know the dilemma of being in the human nature and walking in the Spirit. There is a battle that takes place between a person's natural and a person's spiritual. The natural side of man desires to impress other men. This is why we use titles. This is why people go to school and get their degrees and their skills. They set goals of how they are going to live and they use examples of how other people live as that idea of how they want to live.

Solomon says to us, that:

"The eye is never full of seeing."

No matter what, you can go out today and buy yourself a 2013 Maserati. The 2014 will come out next year with more bells and with more whistles. It will look prettier. And here you are stuck with a 2013 — stuck. Now you would think that is a nice place to be stuck, but the person with the 2013 looking at the 2014 is feeling,

"Aw man, I should have waited."

We go through this throughout the course of our lives. The point is that when you desire and you determine that you are going to live a Spirit-filled, Spirit-led life, it has a tendency to have things come out of your mouth that contradict the desires that you have in your heart in the natural.

I think many of us desire to live comfortably. We desire to live in certain neighborhoods. We want to get away from the riff-raff. We want to raise our children in comfortable settings. Some of us like going on vacation. We like seeing the world. We like going on cruises. We like people thinking that we are important. We like being in the company of other important people. We like a lot of things. I think that is human nature.

But when it comes down to the things of the Spirit, those human desires can get in the way of the things that Father desires for us. The final part of this teaching today is going to bring us all to a point where we have to make a decision.

I believe personally that you can have both. I believe you can have both the success in the natural and have a solid Spirit-led relationship with the Almighty. But the issue is the order. That is the issue. This is why I believe Yeshua said that we have to put first things first. We have to seek first the Kingdom of YeHoVaH.

I was thinking just over the course of this week, where this path has brought me. Four years ago I was on the track of being able to write my own ticket in religion. I had the pension plan. I had the education for my children. I could name the job, the city, the state — well not the job, but the pastorate. I could name what city, what state, what country that I wanted to put my invitation for a call to take on a pastoral congregation. That is the track that I was on.

I went from having the ability, and you have to understand something folks. I understand how to exploit, which is another thing. As a Black man in a Christian-Reformed Dutch congregation, I was a hot item because there wasn't "a whole lot of me."

Every denomination out there desires to have people of color that they can put up as the poster child — and look at what we are doing. We've got Blacks. We've got Hispanics. We've got Asians. We are a multicultural denomination. I was one of those rare things: a Black man teaching Dutch Reformed. It was the same thing in the Lutheran Church. I had the ability to go wherever I wanted. I went from that to not knowing how I was going to feed my family.

For a man who wants to provide, that is a tough place to be. I couldn't tell my family that we had no money. I smiled. I went on like everything was fine. But crying out to the Father every moment — walking away from what looked like — to people who saw this, they felt,

> "Man you must be losing your mind. What's wrong with you? You've got everything. I mean, you are rubbing elbows with people we can't even get to. How do you do this? How do you do that?"

All of the time it was the Father leading me into these places. This is what I believe the Father does.

You see for me, I know exactly where it started. It started when I was around 10 or 11 years old. I started hearing this voice that I didn't understand. I didn't know it. I didn't know about Samuel. I didn't know about Eli. I didn't know the story about Samuel hearing the voice and going to Eli. I didn't know any of that because I was Baptist. I learned this later on in the Baptist when I decided to go back and rededicate my life. I learned that Father tried to communicate with this young man and he didn't recognize the voice of the Almighty.

Over the course of my life I can distinctly remember this voice speaking to me. I remember it while I was out doing things I know I shouldn't have been doing. I remember it when I was trying to get drunk, trying to get high, trying to drown my problems in the bottom of a glass. To me the only real glass of alcohol was an empty one. I knew this voice.

When I went to rehabilitation; before I went to the rehab, I went to a 21-day program. I was there for 17 days and they told me,

"You can go home now."

But I knew when I went there that I wasn't going to be there long because before I went, my mind was already made up. This was the direction the Father was leading me. In this rehabilitation center I remember distinctly that the voice showed up and began to tell me that I had become just like my dad.

In this process, the things that I liked about my dad, and the things that I despised about my dad had become part of who I had become. Things that I didn't want to be, things that I didn't want to inherit from him, I inherited. And it happened by default.

David talks about how he was raised in — he was born in sin and raised in iniquity. The way I interpret that is that our environment has a way of dictating our path. If we don't like the path that we see from the environment that we are in, then we need to change that environment.

This is what motivates parents to move their children out of troubled neighborhoods into a more stable neighborhood to get out of the urban community to go to the suburban community or into the rural community. They don't want the impact of the environment to shape their children; which is now going to determine how they think and how they relate and even where they end up.

When I read about David talking about how he was born in sin and shapen in iniquity, I hear that in my own life. In my household, how I grew up is what shaped me. Even things that I hated, I had become. Things that I despised had become a part of who I had become. The Father shows up in that rehabilitation center and He says,

"You've become just like your Dad."

And this is what you have to do. Whether we accept this or not folks, we have two parents. We've got our earthly parents. We've got our natural parents and we have our Father which is in heaven. When Yeshua makes the statement,

> "Who is My mother? Who is My brother except they that do the will of My Father?"

He wasn't discounting His mom. He was saying that:

> "My purpose is not to satisfy my mother or my brother, but my Father who is in heaven."

When we make the decision that we are going to walk with our Father who is in heaven, often times that is going to put us at odds with our earthly parents, and that becomes a problem for us on a human level.

This is what causes people to be stuck in ruts that they know they don't want to be in — don't like being in. And they refuse to make the decision to walk with the Father because they don't want to leave their natural parents. We see the Patriarch Abraham. The first thing Father says to him that we know of is,

> "Abraham, in order for you to have the relationship that I desire to have with you, you are going to have to leave your father's house."

So Father shows up. He begins to show me that I had become like my earthly dad and that the only way that I was going to overcome this was that I was going to have to go through a process of denunciation. Here I am in a rehabilitation center. I don't know anything about deliverance. I don't know anything and I am making statements and declarations because Father is saying,

"You need to denounce this."

"I denounce my blood line. I denounce my father. I denounce my family. I denounce all worldly connections."

This is the stuff that is going on in my room in a rehabilitation center in Spring Lake, Michigan. Nobody is there but me and the Holy Spirit, which I really didn't know at the time.

Coming out of that, it set me on a path. Now I have to determine how I'm going to live my life. I'd love to tell you that after that situation happened, everything went well. It didn't. Now in that revelation that I am coming to know the Father, there are some things that are stirred up in me — things that I didn't care about before, now become very, very important to me. The number one thing is that I was going through a divorce. What was important to me was that I wanted my wife back.

I felt that my life could not move forward until she was back in my life. That is how I felt. I don't know why I felt that way. My father was a divorcee. My mother was a divorcee. No one in my family — no one in my family was married, that both spouses didn't work. I knew as a young man that when I got married, my wife was not going to have to work outside of the home — unheard of. I knew.

The only stay-at-home moms that I knew when I was growing up were mothers who could not find a job. But I knew and I don't even know where this came from; that my wife was not going to work for somebody else. I don't know where it came from. It was part of who I was.

I am the youngest of eleven children. All of those who were married — both the husband and the wife worked. Everybody worked. My mom worked. My dad worked. But I knew that is not what I wanted. I don't know where it came from at the time. I know where it came from now.

Here I am in my room in my apartment around the corner from my wife's apartment. I couldn't come 500 yards within her presence because she had taken out a restraining order against me. So I moved 500 and I think five feet away. I could step out of my backyard and see her backyard and she could see the same.

In that room I remember several times that I wanted to take my life. I remember one particular time that I was actually thinking about how to commit suicide to the point where I was going to actually do it. Life had gotten so terrible. Now this is after going through deliverance in a rehabilitation center.

I did something really strange. I picked up the phone and I called my brother who doesn't go to church. He was a career Navy man. I don't know if you know about career Navy men. But I think that they curse more than any other Armed Force branch. I mean every other word out of his mouth was a swear word. I called him and told him what was going on in my life and what I was thinking about doing, and he says,

"You need to bury yourself in your church."

This is what my brother said to me. The next Sunday I went back to the Baptist Church. About three months of being in the Baptist Church, I decided I was going to yield to this voice in my head that said,

"Listen. You are to preach My word."

It was at that point — it got to the point where I was so engrossed in what Father was saying for me to do, that I noticed that the desire for my wife was not as great as it once was. The things that I put in front of Him — I said that if He would give me my wife back, I would do what He said. But the relationship began to develop to the point where my relationship with Him began to become stronger than the relationship I desired to have with my wife, and that was frightening.

This led me to really wanting to know Him. And now I'm on this journey from the Baptist Church to the Pentecostal Church to the Charismatic Church to the Lutheran Church to the Christian-Reformed Church, to the Independent and the Messianic, to here.

I'm sharing these things with you because what I have come to realize is that if I am going to follow and do what I believe He is telling me to do, like Jeremiah, I can't look at the faces of people. I can't be so concerned about the things that I desire as much as the things that He is telling me to do — knowing that every time I stand and minister, that somebody might like me less.

That is the price we pay. You will pay a price. And so going through this process of learning how to hear the voice of the Almighty, I have come to realize that most people don't want to hear Him. The reason why most people don't want to hear Him is because they are not willing to make the sacrifice that would be required in order to follow Him.

This is why the road is narrow. People are unwilling to make the sacrifices. Now I'm not talking about something weird, but the fact of the matter is this. I was just crunching some numbers here. Looking at Christianity as we know it, it has been in existence now for a little over seventeen-hundred years.

Seventeen-hundred years. Seventeen-hundred years and seven billion people on the planet. And less than 37% of the seven billion people after 1,700 years believe that Jesus Christ is the Son of God. The trillions of dollars — 31 Christian networks; 24 hours a day, 7-days of the week, Christian TV is broadcast in every nook and cranny, in every nation on the planet.

Thirty-seven percent — what does that say? That says to us that 62 or 63% of the world's population has either rejected the Gospel of Jesus Christ as the church has preached it, or they are just flat-out heathens and are worshipping other gods.

Now this is 1,700 years. As I looked at what Father is calling us to do, I was thinking that after 1,700 years, two billion Christians, three million, 700,000 churches; 66,000 denominations, and the impact of all of this results in just 37% of the world's population believing that Jesus Christ is the Son of God.

Now where does that put us as individuals who are talking about taking the true Gospel — the unleavened Gospel to the nations of the world? We are so far behind the eight-ball folks, it isn't even funny. You talk about a voice crying in the wilderness? We are a whisper.

In order for the church after 1,700 years of evangelizing — that means that churches had to engage all of their members to hit the streets and to invite people to their churches or to tell people an evangelical message that would get people to ask Jesus Christ into their heart. So when the Father says,

> "I want you to go and take the Gospel to
> the nations of the world,"

I am looking at that and I am thinking,

> "This is overwhelming. How in the world are
> we going to do that?"

He had to remind me. You see, everything goes back to the word. Everything goes back to the word. When we enter into human philosophy and try to make the word fit into our philosophical ways and ideas, then we are now adapting the word to our ideas instead of our ideas being born out of the word.

Yeshua started with twelve folks — twelve. Now 1,700 years later, I guess they are still at it in some way or another. The bottom line is that we have an opportunity to if not reach the seven billion people on the planet through the mediums that the Father has provided, we can reach the 37%. And from that to the other 63%. Now, we can look at the enormity of the problem and get overwhelmed and say,

> "How in the world are we going to do this?"

Or we can look to the enormity of our heavenly Father and say.

> "We can do this."

This is one of the similar situations the children of Israel faced when they were at the edge of the land of promise and they saw the people who caused discouragement and fear to enter into their heart and say,

> "I don't think we can do this."

So each week as I am talking to people, I'm sharing,

> "Hey, we've got an opportunity to take the Gospel to the nations of the world and here is all we need. Here is this amount of money we need to get this equipment."

It's not about the money. It's not about the equipment. It is about the 37%. It is about the 63%. It is about those individuals who need to hear the Gospel — the true Gospel of Messiah to make an informed decision.

Over the last three weeks I have received numerous emails and letters from individuals. One person wrote me and said,

> "Do you know, while you were preaching, all I could do was fall on my face and weep?"

There have been more weeping emails and letters that I have received over the last three weeks than in my entire ministry. We are getting into a sensitive subject — understanding how to hear His voice. And how many of us have heard His voice and shut His voice off because of circumstances, because of life, because of human desires, and because of ambitions?

I want to move through all of this because I've been talking. I want to get to some scripture. Those of you out there, listen. You know we need your support. We need you to give. If you don't give, we won't be able to keep doing what I am doing and what we are trying to do. But you already know that. I notice that when I don't ask people to give, they don't. That is just the nature of people.

> "You have not because you ask not."

So we ask and we keep on asking and we keep on asking. Then people write in and say,

> "You know, if you are doing what God wants you to do, you don't have to worry about that. God will provide."

That is what they say. But He says,

> "Ask and you shall receive. You have not because you ask not."

How do we learn to hear His voice? I believe that with where we are headed, many of us believe that the world that we are living in is not getting better. It is seemingly getting worse. The leadership that we put our trust in — there is gridlock in Congress.

We've got a President that 47% of the nation doesn't want. And by the way people, when you begin to look at the numbers — when you begin to look at the American population, the American population identifies almost 80% as born-again Christians.

When you think about 80%, that means that there are about 20% that are "other." But you've got 80% of people who are born-again Christians. Now, you take those numbers and you put them into different grids and what you will find is that in one of the particular grids in pew research, they ask the nation, the United States of America,

"Who is the most influential Christian leader in America?"

Number one being Billy Graham; number two being Pope Benedict, number three being President Barack Obama. Now people can say what they want. But 80% of the American population, the majority of them are not Evangelicals, which are the smallest sect of Protestant denominations by the way. They say that our President — I call him "ours" because I am an American. Those of you who don't call him your President, maybe you're not an American. But last time I checked, he's the President of the United States.

Now I might not like that, but that is the reality of the matter. I can say I might not like that. I didn't vote for him this time. I did vote for him last time, and I am not ashamed of that, you see. I don't feel like I need to give you a reason for why I do what I do.

You do what you do because of who you are. But 80% of this nation views him as a Christian. Is it any wonder that he was a landslide victory over a Mormon who is not viewed as a Christian? Now we can say what we want, but folks these numbers tell us some serious things.

It tells us what the people in our nation want. Now that doesn't mean that you want that. But if you know what people want and you know what people are after, then it is now a matter of how do you reach those people? They will tell you how to reach them.

So when we look at this population of people that we are living with; that we are living among, these individuals see things a certain way. We can use this information and data. The churches have used this information and data.

Businesses use this information and data. Fortune 500 corporations use data. Why shouldn't we?

The children of this world are wiser than their generation according to scripture, than the children of light. Most of us, if we are not careful, will put our head in a hole. We only want to be part of a small group of people that we can spout off our doctrine to and blow smoke up each other's tallits.

The bottom line is that we need to know how to hear His voice. We can all see the direction that not only this nation, but the world is going in. Whether we like it or not, we can say our economy is in bad shape — that we who are used to 4% GDP is only growing by 2%, when the world around us is not growing at all. Do you hear what I am saying? Now that may not mean anything to you. But the bottom line is data, and this data is what people take to the polls.

This data is what people come to church with. This data is what people come to Messianic fellowship with. You see? Every last one of you has an opinion. You have an opinion about religion. You have an opinion about God. You have an opinion about me. You have an opinion about this building. You have an opinion about the person who sits next to you. You have opinions about everything.

If you let other people's opinions shape who you are, then the question is,

"Who are you following?"

When we want to follow the voice of YeHoVaH, we are going to have to separate ourselves from the opinions of other people. The most influential entity in the earth besides the voice of YeHoVaH, is the opinions of other people.

Whether that person is your spouse; whether that person is your son, your daughter, your mother or your father; their opinions are what shape us. We maneuver through life based on the opinions of other people and what other people think of us. You can deny it, but it is true. Every move you make — you go through your head as to who is going to like it and who is not going to like it and that determines your next move.

Some of us want to do what we want to do. So we cover up our actions because we know that if certain people find out, how they are going to feel about it? We hide it from them. Let me tell you something folks. The cat is out of the bag. Father knows your thoughts. There is not a thought that you have that He doesn't know. He not only knows the thoughts that you have, but He knows the intent. He knows the motivation. He knows the ambition. He knows the things that are dormant; waiting to be awakened (like your Spirit), and He wants to awaken them.

How do we learn to hear His voice? We learn how He speaks. How has He spoken in the past? How many of you can distinctly point to a point where you thought you heard the voice of YeHoVaH? Let me see your hands. How many of you have ever thought? Let me see your hands.

Now you have to understand something. One of the ways Father communicates to us is through our thoughts. That is a huge communication avenue — thoughts that you think that you are having that may or may not be your own thoughts. Where are they coming from? I can recognize them. How does He speak today? Where does He speak to me? Where have you heard His voice? What is the last thing He said to you? We read in the King James Bible how:

> **Heb 1:1** "God, who at sundry times and in divers manners spake in time past unto the fathers by the prophets,"

> **Heb 1:2** "Hath in these last days spoken unto us by his Son, whom he hath

> appointed heir of all things, by whom also
> he made the worlds;"

What are the ways YeHoVaH has spoken? He spoke at different times in different ways.

1. He speaks through His word.

His word is very much a major, major way. You see, we've got to get away from the idea of,

> "What is the best Bible to read?"

That is a distraction. Find one and read it, you see. I would say find two or three different versions and read them and compare them. Find four or five different versions and read them and compare them. The main thing is that you read. Why? Because when you look at this book as a Bible, you won't see it as YeHoVaH. You see:

He and His word are one.

When you get into the word, you are actually getting into conversation with Him if you read His word with the idea that maybe He might speak to you. Someone said this to me and I will pass it on to you. When you read the Bible, don't worry about trying to understand it. Don't worry about that. Understanding will come.

Here is the challenge, folks. The Bible — the word of YeHoVaH comes from Spirit. Yeshua says,

> "My words are Spirit."

Here we are trying to comprehend spiritual words from a natural mind. The Bible tells us through the Apostle Paul in *I Corinthians* chapter 2 that the natural-minded man does not understand spiritual things because they are foolishness.

This is why 62 to 63% of the world's population do not view this book as valid. It is foolishness to them. Twenty percent of Americans do not view this book as valid. It is

142

foolishness to them. And even among the 80% of those who confess to be Christians, this book is foolishness to many of them. That is His word.

He spoke audibly. He spoke to the children at the foot of the mountain. He spoke through the angel. He communicates through dreams, through visions — to believers and unbelievers alike. He communicates through His written word. He communicates to His people by His Spirit. And this piece here is where it gets a little tricky. His Spirit is invisible. It is not involving someone else. It involves you and your natural mind and your Spirit mind. You say,

"Well, you've got a Spirit mind?"

Yes you do. You see, in our natural mind, we were born with it. Our Spirit-mind, we were born-again with it. When you are born from above, you are born of the Spirit. Your natural body continues to decay. You continue to get old. You continue to get gray and wrinkled.

And let me tell you something folks. You can do whatever you want to do, but time will catch up with you. You can buy a toupee. You can get hair transplants. You can get liposuction. You can get Botox. You can scrape here and skim off a little there. You can do all of that stuff, but the question is,

"Why? Why are you doing it?"

Because you are concerned about how other people see you. Folks say,

"Well, I'm not doing it for that, I'm doing it for myself."

Well then why are you in the mirror? You are concerned about how you see you. If you are concerned about how you see you, you are concerned about how others see you. You want to see yourself right before you

143

present yourself to other people unless you do this and you become a hermit and move into the mountains. Folks who move into the mountains don't necessarily care about how they look.

There are billions and billions of dollars to be made on makeup and hair products and surgery — cosmetic surgery; all of that stuff. I think the sooner we understand that we are concerned about how people think about us, the more quickly we can get to the point where we decide what matters most — what others think or what He thinks.

He communicates to us by His Spirit. He is going to communicate to you by your Spirit; not your natural mind. This is why you know, when I am hearing Him, to my natural mind I am looking to see who is calling me. I am hearing a voice. I'm thinking I'm hearing this voice through my ears. But get this. I'm the only one who hears it. These people around me, they don't hear it. So if I am hearing it, it is obviously not natural because the natural people around me would hear it too, you see.

When the Father communicates to you, even though at times it may seem audible, it is not audible to other people. He is not talking to you audibly in the natural as much as He is speaking through the Spirit to your spirit.

Even before you were born-again, you still had the image and likeness of YeHoVaH residing in you. It is He who comes along and quickens your spirit so that your spirit may now be able to commune with His Spirit.

As we are filled by His Spirit, we are not led by our spirit. But we are led by His Spirit leading our spirit and which is taking dominion over our natural realm. Now I know I just said a mouthful, but I think you get it.

This is our problem. We live in two worlds. We live in the spirit realm and we live in the natural realm. The problem is that we can't see the Spirit. We can't see it. And when we begin to talk to the Spirit in the company of others who don't hear the Spirit talking to us, we look crazy.

"Who are you talking to?"

YeHoVaH communicates to His people by His Spirit, through the five-fold ministry. Now some of you have heard of this five-fold ministry. The five-fold ministry as it is dubbed in Charismatic circles, is this:

1. **Apostles**
2. **Prophets**
3. **Evangelists**
4. **Pastors**
5. **Teachers**

This is found in the book of *Ephesians*. In *Ephesians* chapter four verse seven, it says:

> **Eph 4:7**   "But unto every one of us is given grace according to the measure of the gift of Messiah."

Every one of us.

> **Eph 4:8**   "Wherefore he saith, When he ascended..."

And let me just back up a little bit because this is a very powerful, powerful verse if you can see it. It says:

> "...unto every one of us is given grace according to the measure of the gift of Messiah."

So now what we are seeing is that based on your ability to receive or your willingness to receive, it will determine how much He gives you. Remember the parable about the Master who went off to a far away land and he called his servants? He gave one of them a talent. He gave another two talents and he gave another five talents.

Remember the **Maximizing Your Talents** message? The one who had the one talent buried his talent in the ground.

And the one who had two talents went out and doubled his talents. The one with five talents went out and doubled his. And the Father took; or the Master when he returned, took the talent from the one and gave it to the one who had five.

You see, based on what you do with what Father gives you, will determine how much He gives you. If you are faithful over the little — and if you were to take this in the Spirit; take this out of the physical realm and take it into the spirit realm. If you are faithful in the little bit that He communicates with you in the Spirit, then guess what? He will begin to communicate with you more. He will communicate with you more and more.

I thank the Almighty that Samuel had an Eli. Even though Eli was backslidden, Eli knew enough to tell Samuel that,

> "Wait a minute. This voice that you are hearing is not coming from me. There is nobody else here. So it must be God speaking to you. The next time you hear this voice, this is what you do."

So the next time Samuel heard the voice, he didn't run to Eli saying,

> "Hey, did you call me?"

He said,

> "Yes, YeHoVaH,"

If you would.

> "I'm listening."

Father communicates to us just like He communicated to Samuel. The question is, are we saying,

> "Yes Father, I'm listening?"

Or has life and the needs and the circumstances and the stuff that we are trying to accomplish in life have us so busy running to and fro that we don't have time to stop and listen?

People ask me. They say,

> "I want you to pray. I want you to pray."

I find it hard to pray for people for a job. Now I will pray for them because they ask me.

> "Pray to the Father that I find a job. I have been unemployed and I need a job."

One of the questions that I will ask, depending upon the tone and whether or not I feel I have the liberty to speak to this person, I will ask the person,

> "Well, what kind of job do you want? What do you believe the Father is calling you to do? Have you ever thought about business? I mean, why is it that you need a job? Why are you praying for a job?"

Every last one of us has been given the measure. Father has placed things in us that He wants us to accomplish. I had my plan. This was not it. And you've got yours. Society teaches us to find a job. My daddy taught me. Listen. He said,

> "Two things you want. Two things you want. Two things YOU WANT. You want a good job, and you want a car that is going to get you there."

My life's goals from my Dad were to make sure that I had a good job and a good car. If I had those two things, than everything else in life — you know I could work that and accomplish. But I needed a good job and I needed good transportation. I have always had that in my life.

When He told me to leave the job that I had in which I was looking to go up that ladder like many of us, I had to walk away from that. People thought I was crazy. You are leaving a job. You are leaving medical benefits. You have the best benefits. Listen. My job paid for me to go to school. My job paid for me to go and get my degree. My job paid for me to go to rehabilitation. My job paid me to do training. I had good dental, good medical, good educational benefits and I walked away from that with no benefits.

I see what it means to walk away from things. I've had to walk away from a few things over the course of my life. But the hardest thing was to embrace what I am doing right now. And do you know why it was hard for me to embrace what I am doing right now, if I can just put it out there to you? Because I've never — you know, I identify with Forrest Gump. I'm really not that smart. I felt that there were people much more qualified to do this than me. I felt that there were people who had a much better grasp of English.

I had a brother write me just yesterday. You know, one of my biggest critics in ministry has always been English teachers because they want to correct me. Darren, you think that being from Arkansas is tough, being from Mississippi — you know, because we make up words. We add "S-es" to *Revelations*, "S" to peoples, "S" to fishes, to geeses. You know, we just add "S-es."

And our sentence structure is not all that great sometimes, either; especially when we are talking to people that we know. It's only when we get around people that are more educated that we are much more concerned about how we put a sentence together. And now we sound "proper."

One of the biggest fears I had was talking in front of people. I had to overcome that to do what I am doing. I think most people do. They did some research several years ago and they talked about what are the things people fear most. The fear of speaking in front of people was greater than the fear of death. People would rather die than speak in front of people. That was the conclusion of the research. That is certainly how I felt. So what I had to do was I had to invest in building my vocabulary. I still have work to do, but I had to start.

I used to buy — I have cassettes at home. You know, back when they had the cassettes; I was raised up in the eight-track era. But when they went to the cassettes, man, that was cutting edge! So I have all of these cassettes and one of them was a vocabulary builder. I listened to tapes over and over and over to be able to put proper sentence structure together — and again I am not there yet.

But this is the thing that I had to do to invest in myself to prepare me to do what the Father is calling me to do. And that is a lesson — that you have to prepare yourself for the word, for the work, for the calling that the Father has called you to.

What I tried to do with the Discipleship Training and with creating an atmosphere where if you are looking for praise and worship and all of that stuff, as you notice, we didn't have that. We will have it at some point when the time comes, but that is not what was important.

Most of the people that I know, when I went to seminary or Bible College and went into seminary and to churches, one of the things that was important in church planting is that before you find a pastor, you find a worship leader. A church can do without a pastor, but it cannot do without a worship leader.

Most churches have worship leaders — whether it be hymns that they sing from the piano or from the organ, or whether it be a full-fledged band or an orchestra.

149

Meanwhile they have a pastoral committee looking for a pastor. They can bring hirelings in until they get a permanent hireling.

So, according to the measure of the gift, Yeshua is giving all of us grace. And what you do with what He gives you will determine how much more He gives you. If you are not going to do anything with what He gives you, why would He give you more?

> **Eph 4:8** "Wherefore he saith, 'When he ascended up on high, he led captivity captive, and gave gifts unto men.'"

> **Eph 4:9** "(Now that he ascended, what is it but that he also descended first into the lower parts of the earth?"

> **Eph 4:10** "He that descended is the same also that ascended up far above all heavens, that he might fill all things.)"

Now what is interesting in this particular verse is that the word "fill" there is the very same word in the book of *Matthew*, where it talks about how:

> "He came not to abolish the law or the prophets, but to fulfill."

It is the same Greek word, "*pléroó*" (pla-ro'-o). And if you notice, there are several words that people have a tendency to gravitate toward when they see this word "fulfill." One of the areas that they will gravitate to is "complete" or "expire." Where is that at? End! He didn't come to abolish the Law. He came to "end" it! That is the way a lot of them interpret this verse.

There are a lot of words, and it depends upon the content, because also in there it is to "execute an office" — to "fully preach," to "perfect," and these words make more sense. The bottom line is that what was being preached at the time was not the Torah, but man-made rules and regulations that are referred to as the "traditions of men." He said,

> "These people worship Me in vain because they are teaching the traditions of the elders and making My law of no effect."

This is what He said. Verse 11 of *Ephesians* 4:11, And He gave some:

1. **Apostles**
2. **Prophets**
3. **Evangelists**
4. **Pastors**
5. **Teachers**

And so you see five gifts there.

> **Eph 4:12**   "For the perfecting of the saints,"

Now understand something. The work of the Messiah is still being done. Yeshua could have come and done everything that needed to be done and was done — the Kingdom established, the enemies of YeHoVaH destroyed, and Yeshua sitting on the throne and reigning. Instead he allowed those who persecuted him to hang him on a stake. He empowered the twelve whom he had chosen and left them there with a particular message:

> "Make disciples."

Somewhere around 300 A.D.; maybe 200 A.D., the message got switched into getting people saved. It was moved from *making disciples* to *evangelism*. Evangelism was never for the purpose of trying to get people to say a prayer asking Jesus to come into their heart. Evangelism —

and you will notice that when these individuals went out to evangelize, they spent time and they planted ministries.

They taught them the things that Yeshua taught. They didn't go preaching *about Yeshua*. They went preaching *about the Kingdom.* It is about the Kingdom of Heaven — the Kingdom of God. It was about:

> "How do you live your life according to YeHoVaH's plan in His Kingdom?"

When you find the calling and the purpose of your life, you won't be like the children of Israel wandering in the wilderness. You will know what it is you are called to do.

The only way you are going to know what you are called to do is to develop this relationship with the Father so that you can hear His voice so that He can tell you why you are here. I can't tell you that. I can help you discern it. I can help you identify your gift set. I can help you identify your areas of strengths and weaknesses and I can affirm once you say,

> "This is my calling."

I can affirm that based on an assessment. But to tell you, unless the Father speaks to me and tells me,

> "This is what this person is supposed to do."

And that has happened. So here we see that Yeshua gave gifts. He gave individuals as gifts for the perfecting of the saints. You see, it's not the responsibility of the apostles, profits, evangelists, pastors and teachers to do the praying; to take the good news to the world. Our responsibility is to equip. I will show you this.

> **Eph 4:12** "For the work of the ministry, for the edifying of the body of Messiah:"

Eph 4:13 "Till we all come in the unity
of the faith,"

Every last one of us. And until we all come:

"...and of the knowledge of the Son of God,
unto a perfect man,"

See, Father is calling you to be a perfect person. That
doesn't mean that you are going to do everything perfectly.
But you are perfect to Him in understanding who you are in
Him — understanding that in the natural you are going to
make all kinds of mistakes. But when you learn to depend
upon the Spirit and leading by the Spirit, He is going to test
you. He is going to take you into places. He is going to
prove you to see if you will keep His commands. He is
going to prove you to see if you are going to run off.

Now that you understand your purpose, will you do
your own thing and build your own Kingdom and make a
name for yourself? Or are you going to be about His
business? That is what is most important.

Solomon knew. Come on folks. Solomon had
everything any of us could ever hope to have. This man had
so much gold and silver, he had it in piles behind his
palaces.

You have these little Messianics out there talking about
polygamy — having more than one wife. Solomon had
seven hundred concubines — 300 of them wives. And he
came to the conclusion that there is only one purpose. The
whole duty of man is to *fear God and keep His commands.*
That's all. FEAR Him and keep His commands. Father
showed up at the Mt. Sinai and said that He came to prove
them that they might FEAR Him and keep His commands.
Now we see here that:

Eph 4:13 "Till we all come in the unity
of the faith, and of the knowledge of the

Son of God, unto a perfect man, unto the
measure of the stature of the fulness..."

And here is that word again.

"...of Messiah:"

But this is an off-shoot, which is *play'ro-mah,* and that
is to fulfill — to be filled up. He wants you to be filled up
with Him, not filled up with you. This is what John the
Baptist was talking about; or Johanan the Immerser when
he said he must decrease so that Messiah increases.

Eph 4:14 "That we henceforth be no
more children,"

The whole duty of man is
to fear God and keep His commands.

Now the book of *Hebrews* says that at some point we
are supposed to be teachers. You see, it's not the will of the
Father that you all come here and sit for years listening to
me. This is training. Your ministry, your calling, your
platform is wherever you go, you see. You are in a building
doing work; surrounded by I don't know how many people.
It probably has security.

Even if I went in, I probably couldn't get into certain
areas because you have to have some kind of password or
some kind of security to get in there. Then there is security
on the perimeter, so you just can't come out there and set
up your evangelistic tent and do a crusade. You have the
password to get in. When you go in, you are doing a
service, but you are representing Him.

You see, every last one of you, when you go into your
place of business, your place of employment, everywhere
you go, the world is your pulpit. The world is your stage,

and you have opportunities to share what the Father has put in you — not just the word. You say,

"Well not just the word?"

No! Listen folks. When Father gives you abilities, sometimes those abilities are to go inside technology and to figure out how to build it and make it work.

"So how is that the Father giving me that?"

Well, because Father knows that technology is going to break, and the people who have the technology that breaks, don't know how to fix it. So He has specialists go in and fix them, but they have the message that the person needs to hear. And they need to look for the opportunity and be in tuned to His voice.

Listen to me folks. When you look at the world's population, over 50% of Americans who have been married are divorced — over 50 percent. What does that mean? Before a person goes through a divorce, they have marital problems. People are sitting up in these jobs and they are coming in and hiding behind their computer.

They don't want to go home to face that wife or that husband. They would rather be here at work. Some people get away from home to the job. That is their refuge. That is their place of peace. In the place that I worked, they did a survey. It wasn't just in this place, but it was in corporate America. In corporate America what they found is that almost 90% of the people in corporate America were doing a job they didn't want to do.

That is astonishing. Over 70% of them would rather be in some organization where they felt they were literally helping people. Most of these individuals were working jobs making somebody rich. They weren't having an impact on society. They weren't having an impact on people. They weren't helping people's live get better.

And longing within them was a desire to help people, which is why many people in corporate America find some way to volunteer themselves in somebody's non-profit organization. It makes them feel good about themselves. They are giving. They are helping somebody. Most of us have the desire to help other people, but we are too busy working because we have bills that we need to pay and we need the money.

Father is saying,

> "Listen. There are some skills that I will give you that will make you money and free you to do what I am giving you the skills to do, so that you can do My will in the process. I am giving you these skills to get you into places to some of these people that nobody else is going to reach."

They don't have access. Father gives us access, but he gives us a message. Then He wants to get us to a place where we can hear Him so that when He speaks to us to communicate the message, we are not spouting off our doctrines.

There are too many people who are talking heads for religious denominations, who have learned the Roman Road, who have learned Evangelism Lifestyle Way, who have learned these procedures and to communicate with people based upon these procedures. Father says,

> "Listen. No, no no. What you need for this person is a word from Me. I know exactly where they are. I know exactly what they are dealing with. I know exactly what they are going through. I know exactly what is causing them to put that smile upon their face when inside they are probably looking

out the window of their 80th floor penthouse, trying to figure out how to jump head-first."

It is amazing. When the stock market crashed, people died. It was self-inflicted death. Most people kill themselves because they don't want to do what God says. You say,

"Well, how do you know that?"

What would make a person kill themselves? They have come to a place where they are ready to quit. You don't think for a moment that Father knows where they are? You don't think for a moment that Father has tried to communicate to them? They see their situation as impossible — even God can't fix it. And we've got the good news to say,

"Yes He can!"

Can you imagine,

"Honey, have you got that note? Can you please bring it?"

Some of you have heard me say over the course of my life, there have been times when the Father has specifically spoken to me and I stepped out on what He said. Now I am not going to read the names, but I wanted to read this because you have heard me say that I have spoken to people, and some people have told me flat-out that I was off.

There have been times when I think I may have been off a little bit. But even in that, Father — the Bible says that He works together for our good. I will never forget one time as an Elder in a ministry. We had a special meeting because the music minister was an Elder in the ministry.

But the music minister was having sex with one of the musician's wife.

It just broke my heart to see how the ministry was dealing with it. What the ministry wanted to do was ship this Elder off to another congregation and get him out of that environment. But see, if this minister, this Elder, this music minister had adultery in his heart, you could send him away from here, but he'll just commit adultery with someone else's wife somewhere else. I wasn't thinking about this. I remember. Some people may remember, and some people may say,

"That is a violation of confidence."

I wasn't sworn to confidentiality in this situation. But here is what happened. I am sitting there talking. I am in an environment where the man whose wife was committing adultery with the Elder was talking as if this was somebody else. And I told him,

"No man. That is your wife."

Ouch. Fortunately they are still — I think they are together. I was young; immature. It was a dumb move. But do you know what it did? It brought all that mess out into the open. Now they couldn't hide it. They had to force — they were forced to deal with something they were trying to hide, and forced to deal with other issues. That exposed that the pastor was having sex with an Elder's wife.

So there is all this sex going on in this Charismatic, Apostolic Faith "We hear from God move in the Spirit" places. And I wanted to know what part of God told you it was okay for you to commit adultery with the Elder's wife?

I need to know that. I mean, what spirit are you listening to? You are hearing from the spirit. If you are hearing from the spirit, how can you be doing that? That doesn't make sense to me. Now I'm naive. There have been times when I've hidden behind that naiveté, but I wasn't hiding. I am sincerely and genuinely wanting to know.

You are called by God. You claim to be a man of God. You claim to hear from the Spirit. You are prophesying to people. You are casting out devils in people. You are laying hands on people. People are getting well. But you are committing adultery with the Elder's wife and then you are roving the streets for prostitutes at night. I want to know what part of God is leading you to do that? Now that wasn't prophetic, it was pathetic — both what I did, and what they were doing, but Father used it.

The Bible says that the Father will take every situation — all things will work together for our good. Now for me, that hindered a promotion, but it didn't stop the promotion. Three months later I was promoted to Associate, Assistant Pastor to the Pastor. Well not three months, Yeah. It set me back three months in my promotion.

But here is the thing. Promotion doesn't come from the East. It doesn't come from the West. It comes from Him. Do you hear what I am saying folks? Sometimes we are afraid to express ourselves for fear that it is going to get in the way of the track we have laid out.

Another situation about which you have heard me talk, is that we were running a non-profit. A young lady came in with her lesbian mate. I didn't know. The Spirit of YeHoVaH came upon me to prophesy to her. I prophesied to her and she said to me,

> "Preacher, you are so far off."

And then her mate said,

> "Why are you lying to the preacher? I'm her partner. And that preacher just told you about yourself."

Three weeks ago we were here and I knew just as clearly, because I recognized His voice. Father said,

"There is someone here who is having this excruciating back pain."

So I stopped and I called it out, and nobody responded. I gets home, I get home. You see, I just put that "s" on gets. (Laugh) I will put an "s" on a word. You all just please forgive me. I catch myself from time to time. (Laugh) So I get home and I get a phone call from a sister who is probably online; who called her mother who was not online, and she said,

"That was me."

I'm thinking to myself,

"Okay, I'll take that."

But how can someone who is not online hear this word that I am speaking? And I'm asking,

"Who is that?"

Do you remember that day? I said,

"Who is that?"

And nobody raised their hand. The next day, Sunday, I get a phone call from a brother in Georgia. And he said,

"When you said that word, it was for me. I was online and you know, God healed me. I just called you to let you know."

And I said,

"Wow."

So now there's somebody in Texas, and now somebody has called from Georgia. And yeah, I'll take that because it says to me that I didn't miss it. But then this week I get this letter. It said:

Arthur, the Sabbath I was there with my sons. At the end of service, you were praying and paused and asked if anyone in the service was having back pain. When we walked out to our cars, my son, one of them asked me,

"Can that preacher read minds?"

And so I asked, "Why?"

And he said,

"Because he described my back pain exactly how I felt."

I said,

"It was bothering me to the point that I couldn't hardly pay attention to what was being said."

Now he didn't have to send this, but what it did, was Father just wanted me to know that,

"No, you heard Me. See, the person that I was speaking about was sitting right here."

Now why am I sharing this? There are times when you may not see the response. But you have to be confident in the fact that you heard the Father's voice. That comes by exercising your faith in Him and following the leading that He is giving you even though you don't know whether or not it is Him.

When Father began to share with me about stepping out and saying things, I had the same fear.

"Well, what if I am wrong? What if I mess up? What if I don't say it right? What if somebody takes what I say and runs with it? I don't want to hurt people. I don't want to say the wrong thing. I don't want to get people shipwrecked. I don't want to get people off-course. I don't want to be the reason why somebody walks away from you."

And those things will cause you to back off and not do anything.

"You have to be 100% sure!"

Let me tell you something. You will NEVER be 100% sure until you have walked with Him for a period of time — following. There have been times when I am driving, and I hear the voice say,

"Turn here."

And I turn. Do you know how we found this place? Some of you know that a year ago in August, we were told that we had one month to move. People were saying,

"Where are we going?"

"I don't know."

"Where are we going?"

"I don't know."

"We've got to get out of here."

"Well, where are we going?"

"I have no idea."

I was driving down this street. And Father says,

"Turn here."

I passed it, because when He said,

"Turn here."

I'm in the right lane going down just like I normally go when I'm going. You know. How many of you — you've got the same way you go every time you go to the place you go to? How many of you have gone into your car and your car goes into automatic pilot? How many of you who planned to turn at this exit, but because you are so accustomed to going this way, you pass the exit that you are supposed to turn onto?

You see, we get into such a pattern where we do the same thing every day. Every day we get up. We scratch the same place. We yawn the same way. We go to the bathroom. We do this and then we do that, and then we do that. And then we get in our car and our car — I mean we could doze off at the wheel of our car if it was automatic and it would take us the same way to work and the same way home. We do it automatically.

Why? Because you have done this so many times where it just becomes automatic. This is where Father wants to get us — to where we walk with Him for so long that it just comes automatically. As we are moving forward folks, I think about the time when Father wants to communicate to us in such a way where we just follow. We just follow His lead.

He's told me to do things and I get to where I am supposed to — I'm thinking I'm supposed to be. I am sitting there and I am waiting and I don't see anything. I don't hear anything. There have been times when He has told me to do something and then I am watching the news. Come to find out that the path that I am on, if I hadn't turned, I probably would have been in the pile up or the accident, or I don't know.

That is the sensitivity that the Father desires to have with you.

Eph 4:14 "That we henceforth be no more children, tossed to and fro, and

163

carried about with every wind of doctrine, by the sleight of men, and cunning craftiness, whereby they lie in wait to deceive;"

Eph 4:15   "But speaking the truth in love, may grow up into him in all things, which is the head, even Messiah:"

Eph 4:16   "From whom the whole body fitly joined together and compacted by that which every joint supplieth, according to the effectual working in the measure of every part, maketh increase of the body unto the edifying of itself in love."

As we see, here we have a body ministry that is building the body up. So, we find that:

8. YeHoVaH communicates to His people also by His Spirit through all of His people.

Paul wrote in the book of *Corinth*,

"...howbeit brothers when you come together, that each one of you has a hymn or a psalm or a tongue or a prophecy, or interpretation."

You see, Father expects that every last one of us — and this is why the fellowship is so important. When we talk about the healthy congregation, there are four pillars that I believe are important. There is the *Apostles' doctrine*, the *prayer*, the *breaking of bread*, and the *fellowship*. Fellowship is essential. People who are outside of fellowship are left to their own devices.

This is why you have a lot of the internet ranting, I think. You have people who are isolated and are in

164

environments where they don't have fellowship with other people. The internet cyberspace is their world. They can confront. They can be mean. They can put all their words in CAPS. You don't know them from Adam because they are using a screen name and you have no idea who you are dealing with. Why are you arguing with somebody on the internet and you don't even know who they are? Why?

"Well, I just couldn't let them get away with it."

Who?

"Them!"

Who is it?

"I don't know."

YeHoVaH communicates to His people by His Spirit through all of His people. He communicates to you by others, just as He will communicate to others by you. Here is an example.

Ac 8:1 "And Saul was consenting unto his death."

Here we see that Stephen has been stoned. *Acts* chapter 8:

"And at that time there was a great persecution against the church which was at Jerusalem; and they were all scattered abroad throughout the regions of Judaea and Samaria, except..."

Who? Everybody went except the Apostles. Now this is *Acts* chapter 8. When you think about it in *Acts* chapter 1, Yeshua told the disciples — the Apostles at the time, he says,

"I want you to go to Judaea, you start. You go to Jerusalem, Judaea, Samaria, and to the outermost parts of the world."

Father brings a great persecution and the Apostles still won't leave. Now sometimes we don't want to see this about the Apostles, but the Apostles were stuck. They were stuck in Jerusalem when Father had told them to leave. And a great persecution comes where people are being beheaded. People are being killed and they still won't leave.

Ac 8:2 An devout men carried Stephen to his burial, and made great lamentation over him."

Ac 8:3 "As for Saul, he made havoc of the..."

Messianic community, the congregation, the ekklesia...

"...entering into every house,"

Dragging men and women...

"...women committed them to prison."

Because of their faith.

Ac 8:4 "Therefore they that were scattered abroad went everywhere..."

Who? They. Who is they? It wasn't the Apostles. It was you. They went preaching everywhere — the word — everywhere they went.

Ac 8:5 "Then Philip went down to the city of Samaria, and preached Messiah unto them."

> **Ac 8:6**   "And the people with one accord gave heed unto those things which Philip spoke, hearing and seeing the miracles which he did."

Who was Philip? Philip wasn't an Apostle. He was a Deacon — believed to be one of the seven that were chosen. I want you to see something else. When Philip went down,

> **Ac 8:7**   "For unclean spirits, crying with loud voices, came out of many that were possessed with them: and many taken with palsies, and that were lame, were healed."

> **Ac 8:8**   "And there was great joy in that city."

Acts chapter 21, here we see another situation with Philip.

> **Ac 21:8**   "And the next day we that were of Paul's company departed, and came unto Caesarea: and we entered into the house of Philip the evangelist,"

Obviously the one spoken of in *Acts* chapter 8.

> "...which was one of the seven; and abode with him."

And there we see that he was a Deacon. He was an Evangelist. He did the work of an Evangelist. They laid hands on him as a Deacon. He wasn't an Apostle. He was chosen by people who identified that this is a man that is full of the Holy Spirit. Can you say that about the person next to you?

There have been a couple of situations, and I might as well touch on this while I am at it. There have been a couple of situations. I've been in several different churches and several different denominations and I've seen several different ordination processes.

Here is what I have seen, even though all of the processes of ordination were different. The choosing of those individuals who were being ordained was the same. People chose them and they were chosen by personality, familiarity and popularity. I remember when we first decided that we were going to test this theory. In Grand Rapids, Michigan we decided okay, we're going to have Elders. We're a small congregation.

You have to understand. In the days of *Acts*, they started out with 120 and twelve Apostles. Three thousand were added. By the time they chose seven men as Deacons to serve tables, there were thousands of people in fellowship and in attendance. And they said,

> "Listen, you all choose from among yourselves, seven men full of wisdom and full of the Holy Spirit, for it is not fitting that we should leave prayer and the word to serve tables."

So we see that Deacons were chosen to serve tables. Now they are running congregations. They are hiring and firing Pastors. But the criteria was that these men be full of wisdom and full of the Holy Spirit. Every process that I've seen in every environment that I have been in, people chose people by personality, familiarity and by popularity. The Holy Spirit is not even involved in the process.

We decided that we were going to choose some Deacons. It was the same thing, same thing. And now people have a title of Deacon and they want to run things. They want to run people. They want to control. These men

168

were not like that. They understood what they were supposed to be doing. The Apostles understood what they were supposed to be doing. The congregation was growing because everybody was doing what they were supposed to be doing.

> **Ac 21:9** "And the same man had four daughters, virgins, which did prophesy."

Now we don't even know what their names were, but we do know this. They were filled with the Spirit. Why? Because the Bible says that,

> "Your sons and your daughters will prophesy."

> "On My people in the last days; I'm going to pour out My Spirit on all flesh. Your sons and your daughters will prophesy."

And here it is, Philip's daughters. Even though we don't know their names, they were filled with the Holy Spirit. We don't see them with the evidence of speaking in tongues. We see them doing what they are supposed to do when they are filled with the Spirit, and that is to *prophecy*.

I can't tell you how many people that will tell me that they are filled with the Spirit, but they will not prophesy. Do you know what prophecy is? Prophesying is simply this. Father is speaking to me and now He is instructing me to speak to someone. I'm hearing His voice and I'm speaking what He says. That's simple. The heavens didn't open. The angelic choir didn't sing. Doves didn't fly out of the clouds. They just simply prophesied and we don't know who they are.

Every last one of you who claim to be — how many of you are filled with the Spirit? Sons and daughters shall prophesy. Before you prophesy, you have to hear. You have to hear. Hearing the voice of YeHoVaH requires the desire to hear Him speak. You would be amazed at how many people don't believe Father will speak to them. Some of you may be here. I'm here to tell you that is not true. It's not true.

Every last one of you in this room — every one of you on computers, every one of you who will see this message on *YouTube*, you have the ability to hear the voice of YeHoVaH and to speak what He says. But you have to first have the desire to do it. If you don't have the desire to do it, it's not going to happen.

If you are convinced that He is not going to speak to you, He won't. But He will; you just won't hear Him. He has spoken to you. He has spoken to you many times, just like Samuel. You just didn't recognize His voice. I don't believe there is a human being on the planet — especially one who is born-again or one whose parents were in some kind of church or denomination who hasn't heard the voice of YeHoVaH. It is a matter of recognizing Him. But you have to have the desire. You have to have the desire to hear Him.

Eric, I don't mean to put you on the spot, but I told you that when you told me, you blessed me the other day. Do you remember what you said to me? Do you mind sharing? Could I get the microphone just for a moment please? Thank you. Give it to Eric. And here is what I am going to do. I am going to test this. Not Eric, Eric is already proven. What did you say to me the other day, about how you were driving?

Audience member Eric:

Okay, so last week I was here and Arthur spoke about driving in the car and turning the radio off and just listening — praying and listening, listening for a word. We went out to dinner Saturday after sundown and I left the house. As I did that, I turned the radio off and I said a quick prayer. I said I am just going to listen.

So I drove. And as I was driving, I saw an area. I am always looking for a permanent place for Michel's ministry at *A Rood Awakening* — a long-term solution where we are not leasing — we have a situation where we own the land. And on the corner of 521 and 160 in South Carolina, there is an office complex. There are signs that say, "build to spec" you know, "purchase land and we'll build," and things like that.

It's a beautiful area and it is convenient. It's like three miles from my house, so I'm always looking for that spot. I drove down there. It's just beautiful buildings and there is a lot of land. So I was able to turn. I listened. I turned the radio off and I listened and I asked for confirmation, not confirmation, I just listened. I drive by that spot a couple times a week and I've been here for four years. It was the second time I have actually driven over there.

Arthur Bailey adds:

And then you begin to envision.

Eric:

Yeah, I did. Now you are really putting me on the spot.

Arthur:

You don't have to give the details, but...

Eric:

Sure. I envisioned a Messianic Training Center where Michael's ministry is; where Arthur's ministry is.

Arthur:

You just start seeing stuff.

Eric:

That's right.

Arthur:

And see folks, so many times — I mean we have all of this noise. We are surrounded by noise. I mean I'm standing here right now and there's noise. I have sat in my house and I can hear electricity running through the wires. How many of you have heard electricity running through the wires? You can hear stuff.

Father wants us to be on this frequency where we are hearing His voice. We hear stuff. But the point is that Father is trying to get us to a place where we will turn off all the noise; turn off the voices, turn off the radio, turn off the CD player, turn off the TV and find a quiet place. Or let Him lead us to a quiet place, or lead us to a place. And then just like He said to Abraham,

> "Abraham I want you to look. Just look up at the sky. Do you see all these stars? That is going to be the number of seeds. You can't even count them."

He took Moses over to look at the land, and to Abraham he says,

> "Look at the land from as far as the eye can see."

Joshua, whatever piece of ground — he began to cause them to envision — to see things through His eyes. You see, Father doesn't see lack. Father doesn't see poverty.

Father doesn't see the limitations that you and I see. He is trying to get us out of looking through our eyes and into seeing things from His perspective — because it will overwhelm you. What He will show you is that He is much bigger than any box you could ever build.

Can you build a building to put in there? I mean we can have a hundred thousand million square feet complex, and it still won't be big enough. We can turn the entire state of North Carolina into one massive warehouse, where all the people in the state of North Carolina gather for worship and it still won't be big enough for the Father. You can't build — we can't build a building big enough. When you look at things from His perspective, He shows you global, not local. Most people have a local mindset of God.

There are many of you in this room, and I dare say to you that if you listen to what I am saying — because these are not my words. I am giving to you what I believe He has given to me. There are many of you who have similar situations just like Eric, and different situations, just over the course of the last two or three weeks. Anybody in here? See? You guys want to share it? Can I get the microphone? And don't worry about it, this is part of how things are going.

Audience member:

Well for me it was my wife and I am sure a lot of people know about that already here, but when I went to the *Chronological Gospels* with Michael Rood, I was in front of my computer. I was having a debate over whether I should go or should not go. And the Father said,

"Go."

And I went. My wife and I reconciled at the *Chronological Gospels*.

Arthur Bailey:

Now imagine if you had not been there. Do you hear what I am saying? Now you have been praying and believing for reconciliation, and here it is that Father is putting in your heart to go some place. He is putting in your wife's heart to go some place. And had either one of you not gone, the divine connection that He has established would not have happened.

I can't tell you how many connections we have missed because we did not heed the voice. Could you pass the microphone? And why don't you let people know who you are so that afterwards they can have fellowship with you?

Audience member:

My name is Paul. It is basically the same story about the *Chronological Gospels*. I didn't have a way to get there. I just stepped out on faith. I felt that the Father was saying to go. So I went, and I met the most important person in my life. And it has just been continuing. He is just constantly speaking to me and He is bringing me along. He is making some changes at work so I can be off. And I just praise Yah for His many blessings. I do hear His voice and it is that small, still voice, and it is just awesome.

Arthur:

Now you were sitting in here, you have come in here a few times, and you were troubled by the fact that you had to work on the Sabbath

Paul:

That is correct.

Arthur:

And we had a conversation. And you decided as I challenged people. You know there are many people who say,

> "Well, I have to work on the Sabbath."

And I say, well, have you asked for it off?

> "Well, no they are not going to give it to me off. They make us always work on the Sabbath."

What happened in that situation?

Paul:

Well, our head manager had presented to our department manager that they wanted us to change our shift, to go in on Sunday night to Thursday night. And they had us put it to a vote and we voted 7-0 to make that change. Now we're just waiting for that to take effect. We are thinking it is going to be toward the end of the month. I will be able to be off on the Sabbath and I'm putting in for the Feast days as well. But it's moving forward.

Arthur:

Now some of you all may say,

> "Well, you're pushing this a little bit, and you are stretching this a little bit."

But see, I believe that because of you, that Father rearranged the entire structure of that company because of the desires of our heart.

Paul:

And thanks to my coworker here, he was the one that was — that told me about the forms. But the Father is working it out even without the forms. So, it's awesome.

Arthur:

And you know, I hear these testimonies. People have not because they ask not. And yes, the young lady you met — we won't get into that. But I was at the *Chronological Gospels* and what you all may not know about me is that I don't miss much, but I saw these two and I said,

> "Okay, is there something you guys want to tell me?"

Because you know, you see people and with some people you can tell that something is there, these are not just friends. This has gone beyond the:

> "Hey, how you doing? It's good to know another Messianic in the faith and I just want to fellowship kind of conversation."

Anybody else who feels that you have heard the voice of the Almighty? Darla?

Audience member Darla:

Last week I was having difficulty hearing and I like to put my Father to the test. Last Sabbath, there was some distortion going on in me in the Spirit realm. The next morning I was having fellowship with a friend in California on the phone and as soon as I got off, I heard so strongly, the voice of my Father. He says that,

> "The body — it's time to get off of the defense and get on the offense."

I didn't really know what that meant, so I got on the internet and looked it up in football terms. This is a game. It is a game of life for His Kingdom, and I am now on the offensive position.

Arthur:

Which is where we are supposed to be.

Darla:

Yes, yes. And I also heard, and I've shared this with some friends who are in this building now, that no matter what we say one to another, Father hears it all.

Arthur:

Everything.

Darla:

Everything whether written or spoken. And He clearly defined to me because I was in a quandary. He told me that Arthur, that before Him, you have a pure heart and I am to expose that to the nations. Because before YeHoVaH, Arthur Bailey, you have a pure heart.

Arthur:

Hallelujah. This young lady behind you, right here. Ma'am, Hi. Yeah. I just wanted to say Hi, I am so glad to see you. You were here a few weeks ago. I felt so strongly that the Father was really speaking to you that He was literally trying to communicate to you in a way, and He was really, He was saving you. Did you sense anything going on the last time you were here?

What is your name if you don't mind? Alicia? I'm glad to see both of you all back again. And please if you don't mind, hang out for a little while. I'd like to get to know you. I'm glad, because when they let you out the door, I asked them why. That is the young lady. It's like,

> "How can you all just let people leave, when
> I know Father has work; He has things that
> He's trying to communicate to them?"

Anybody else feel like a brief moment before I carry on? Yes, my baby. I need you to get the microphone for a minute.

Audience member Marla, Arthur's daughter:

Shabbat Shalom everybody.

Arthur:

Shabbat Shalom.

Marla:

Um, recently I've been hearing from the Father...

Arthur:

What's your name?

Marla:

My name's Marla Dad!

Arthur:

Oh.

Marla:

Laughs. Yeah. So I have been having a lot of struggles with saving my money and not spending it all the time, and you know going from check to check. When I've worked so hard, I shouldn't be living check to check. And I was constantly wondering, why can't I save my money? I'm not spending it like I think I am, but I just couldn't save it.

And so week after week I would come here and the tithes and offerings basket would come around. And I would say,

> "Oh no, I can't do it this time because I've got this or this or..."

Whatever the excuse might be; I would always find one. So a lot of, recently I have been hearing,

> "You need to give your tithes and offerings, that is something you need to do."

It is technically not even yours. You have to give that. It is a requirement of Him. And so for the last three weeks I have been making that a priority. I'm just saving money like crazy now. I'm saving and I'm being able to start doing things that I wanted to do with my money. And I really think that it is because I started giving my tithes and offerings. I just wanted to share that.

Arthur:

Yeah. You know, on that note if you can grab that and we'll give you more opportunity. But I remember — I grew up watching TV because TV was an outlet. In the era when John Dillinger first came out, there were Al Capone movies and gangster movies and all those kinds of things. I want to share this with you because Father speaks to us where we are.

He will use those things that are familiar to us to communicate to us. When my daughter was talking about tithes, I remember the illustration that the Father gave me concerning tithes. You know how in the neighborhood

179

when the people who control the neighborhood come by? What they say is that you need to pay protection money. They would come in and they would say,

> "Okay, you are in our neighborhood. This is our turf. We require a certain percentage for you to be here."

And the issue is, well, what do we need protection for?

> "You need protection from us. That is because if you don't pay this money, you know. You will not be able to stay here in peace."

What the Father revealed to me through those movies, is that the tithe is like protection money.

> "Well, who am I being protected from?"

It is like,

> "You are being protected from Me. It is not yours. It belongs to Me. And when you give it and you get it out of your possession, My protection is on you. When you don't give it, My protection is not on you. So now the devourer comes and he has access to you because My protection — I am not protecting you."

He communicated to me that the tithe was like protection money. But anyway that is another story.

Hearing the voice of YeHoVaH requires discerning how He speaks. One is that you desire to hear His voice. Now you can say that,

> "I want to hear His voice."

I am sure that many of you — Okay, it's like,

"I want to be filled with the Holy Spirit. I want to be filled with the Holy Spirit; speaking in tongues. Okay God, fill me with the Holy Spirit. I'm not filled yet! I'm still not filled! I don't feel the Holy Spirit! Okay..."

Then you hear another message.

"Okay, I want to be filled with the Holy Spirit. Somebody lay hands on me. Somebody pray over me. Fill me with the Holy Spirit! Fill me with — I'm not filled yet! Okay..."

I hear another message. I need to be baptized in Jesus' name.

"Okay. I'm going to go and get baptized in Jesus' name now. I'm going down in the water now. They say that when I come up I'm going to be speaking in tongues. I'm coming up now. I'm out! No tongues!"

Okay. You need to tary.

"I'm tarrying. I'm tarrying God, don't you see me tarrying? I want to be filled with Your Spirit. I'm not filled yet. Well maybe this is not for me."

This is what people said. This is what people said you needed to do. That's what I did. That is what they said to do and nothing happened. I went to the tarrying — I got baptized in Jesus' name. I had people pray over me. They laid hands on me. They did all the stuff. But it wasn't until I got desperate. Without anybody around, it was like,

"Father, now I know You are real, because I have heard you."

But my concept of being filled with the Spirit, regardless to the fact that I am hearing His voice is — isn't that amazing? Here I am hearing His voice, but because I'm not speaking in tongues, I'm "not" filled with the Spirit. I am hearing His voice. He is leading me. He's talking to me. He's communicating to me. He is showing me things. He is doing things on my behalf. It is clear that I have a relationship with Him. But I am not speaking in tongues, so I must "not" be filled with the Spirit.

I got desperate. At the corner of my bed one night, with nobody around, it was like,

"Father, I see it in the Bible, I know it's there."

Here is what the Father showed me. I went from a demand to a humility. Why do you want to be filled with the Spirit, so you can impress people with your tongues? So you can pray in tongues so everybody can hear it?

"Aw, robo-schtick-kay-bey-bey-sheem-bah-lah. Don't my tongues sound like adult tongues!"

(Laughter) Do you know what I'm saying? I mean in circles that I was in, people would impress one another with their tongues.

Father doesn't give us these things to impress people with. He gives us these things so that He can get us to the place that He wants us to be, doing what He wants us to do. Often times He will have us do it in secret because the person we are communicating with is just them and us. It is not on the national stage and there is nobody else around.

We have to get out of the mindset that we have to be in the spotlight — because we don't. At the foot of my bed He filled me with His Spirit. Basically what He did was He gave me the ability to speak in tongues. Now the thing of it is folks, is that I already had it.

You see, when you have the Holy Spirit of the Almighty on you, you have everything. The Father is not withholding anything from any of us. The issue is what is the motive? What is your motive? Why is it you want it? So you can convince other people that you are filled with the Spirit? Why do you have to convince somebody else that you are filled with the Spirit? Why are you always trying to convince other people that you are spiritual — that you have knowledge?

You know the Bible showed me — the other day I was driving and He said,

> "I want you to go home and I want you to look up the words 'puffed up.'"

So I go home. I write stuff down. In my phone I have my little note pad. Sometimes I pull over off of the street. I write it down because I don't trust my mind. I go home and I research it. This happens to me all the time.

I'm at home. I'm looking at puffed up. Knowledge puffs up. Pride. Arrogance. People with knowledge have a tendency to get arrogant. Knowledge puffs up. And they get prideful. Why? Because they are trying to impress people with their knowledge. They are trying to impress people with their ability. They are trying to impress people with their spiritual abilities and powers. Father is not interested in who you — He is saying,

> "Impress Me. And if you impress Me, you are going to do it when nobody else is around."

What Father is looking for is how do you conduct yourself when there is no one else around? It requires discerning how He speaks. That means that you have to get somewhere like Habakkuk, who got something to write with, and he expected. Hearing the voice of YeHoVaH requires discerning where He speaks to you and spending time in that place, prepared to hear Him speak.

So many times many of us in this room have felt the prompting of the Father. Here you are driving and He says,

> "Pull over, I want to talk to you."

> "I don't have time, this is a busy place. I can't pull over."

How many of you have had that voice; that prompting to pull over while you are driving and pray? Come on let me see your hands. Did you do it? See?

There are more of you in this room. Father will lead you. And do you know what He is doing? He is proving you. He is showing you what is in your heart.

> "You say you want Me, but when I try to speak to you, it is inconvenient. You want Me on your terms."

Father says,

> "I don't work like that. If you are going to have Me, it is going to be on My terms. It's not going to be on your terms. And it is going to be when you are most inconvenienced. I am going to test you to see if you really want to know Me like you say you want to know Me."

Hearing the voice of YeHoVaH requires obeying Him when He speaks. You see, the more you obey what He says, the more His voice becomes clear and the more He begins to speak. Every single day of my life I set aside some time for Him to speak to me. This is beyond being in tune with Him every single day.

Now, I can be at home thinking okay, I've got to do this, I've got to do that, I've got to do this. I'm trying to figure it out because the way that Charlotte is set up, I don't want to be all the way over here and then go over here to do something and then go all of the way back here. I try to map my plan out. And in the process of mapping my plan, I am listening to where I am supposed to go first.

Even though I have to do all these things, I can go the same route. Every Monday and Wednesday and Friday I do this. Every Tuesday and Thursday I do this. I want to hear His voice as to where I am supposed to go — how I am supposed to go, what direction I'm supposed to take. Am I supposed to take this route or this route? Am I supposed to go across or around? I want to know.

The reason why I want to know is because I am believing Father to do some things I prayed for,

> "Father I know that the earth is Yours; the fullness thereof. You know the things that I need, and You know who is supposed to meet that need. I need You to cause me to make the connections that I need to make so that I can be about Your business. In order for me to make the connections that I need to make, You need to show me where those connections are. When you reveal to me what direction I am supposed to take to make those connections, now this is the route that I take."

Now you may say well,

> "Really?"

Yes. For me, this is how it works. I remember just as clearly last week I am at home. I am thinking, okay, I need to go over to *A Rood Awakening*.

"Not today."

I need to go over to *A Rood Awakening*.

"Not today, next day."

I need to go over to *A Rood Awakening*.

"Not today."

I had stuff in my truck that needed to go and things that I needed to pick up. And then the Father says,

"Okay, go to ARA."

I go over. Michael is putting on his jacket; getting ready to come over here to meet with me. And it is like Father — it is little things like that, that prove He is making connections. I mean, I make connections like this on a regular basis, folks, trying to be where He wants me to be when He wants me to be there. That means spending time quietly every night; every morning. There is a ritual I go through every morning before I get out of bed.

"Father, this is the day You have made, I shall rejoice and be glad in it."

And I wait. I determine,

"Okay, how do you want me to eat today? Do I fast today? Do I abstain? What do I eat? What do you want me to wear today?"

See, He knows where I am going. There is no point in me putting on a suit when I am going someplace where I am going to get my hands dirty or vice-versa.

"You want Me to make a connection, and this is not a day for me to put on my jeans and my plaid shirt that I like. This is the day, because I'm going to cause you to make a connection, and you need to be prepared for the connection that I am going to make for you today."

Now does He lead me into a connection every day? No, but I look for Him to do that. I look for Him to make a connection every day. If He says,

"I want you to go here; I want you to go there."

I'm going. I'm looking.

"Okay I'm here God, what am I supposed to see while I am here?"

Do you follow what I am saying? This is how He wants us to live. Now when you work a job, you have made a commitment to go into that job and to give them a certain amount of time. That is the contractual agreement you have. They didn't take you on the job to have a Bible study during work hours. You will get fired. Do you hear what I am saying?

Now, if you want to have a Bible study on your break; Bible study at lunch, then that's the time you have. But while you are supposed to be here performing your contractual obligation, this is not the time for you to be trying to convert the coworkers.

The Father wants to lead you just like that. The more we obey Him, the clearer His voice becomes and the more He speaks to us. Now, I want to do some praying for you. Next time we are going to take this into a different gear.

We are going to be talking about walking in the power of the Spirit. It is important because there are too many people doing all of this stuff in the Spirit, but their lives are raggedy. Their lives are not right.

You see, when Father begins to deal with you, do you know what He's going to deal with you first about? Not your wife, not your husband, not your children, not your son, not your daughter. He is going to deal with you about you. You go to Him wanting Him to fix this. And He says,

> "Yeah, we'll get to that. But what I first need to do is to fix you. If I don't fix you, you are going to continue to make a mess of things."

The way things are right now, a lot of what you are going through folks is because of your own doing. Father wants to get us to a place where we are wise as serpents if you would; gentle as doves. And we have foresight and insight so that we can see things that are afar off.

That is the work of the Holy Spirit, to show us things to come. He wants us to make connections and alliances with people — some permanently, some to get us to a certain point. But He is trying to cause us to look long-term not short-term; and make alliances and connections and relationships that are going to help us and us help them to get to the point where YeHoVaH has ordained them to be.

All of us are a connection to something else, just as people in your life are a connection to something else. You have to be able to see those connections for what they are. Father will show them to you.

Sometimes we're trying to get attached to people that Father doesn't want us to be attached to. Some of us are attached to people that Father is trying to get us away from because they hinder the creativity, the ability. They hinder the process. They get in the way. They stop the flow. They shut things down. They are just not a good fit.

Now don't somebody run off and say,

> "Okay, God just spoke to me and told me
> that I am to divorce my husband because
> Pastor Bailey says it is not a good fit."

I am not talking that! Don't put that on me! Some folks will do that, so don't do that to me. I believe that Father can work out whatever situation you are in, if you are willing to work it out. If you are not, so be it.

So, I want to pray. Now we've prayed this prayer before and it bears repeating. Here is what you are going to have to do after the prayer. The prayer is not something supernatural that is going to make this happen for you. Just like Eric and just like some of the others. You are going to have to put these things into practice.

See, some of you all left here last week and you turned the radio on just like you do. It probably came on when you turned the car on. The CD kicked in just as soon as you turned the ignition, you see. You kicked into habitual mode. People kick into habitual mode even on the Sabbath.

> "Okay, it's the Sabbath."

Folks, here is something the Father was revealing to me yesterday, again. That is, you know, there are Messianic Baptists.

> "Wow."

There are Messianic Pentecostals. There are Messianic Charismatics. People come out of denominations into Messianic, but they don't leave the denomination. They bring their doctrine and their approach of YeHoVaH — they just look at the Bible differently. Instead of going to church on Sunday, they go to church on Saturday. They still have a church mentality. Father is trying to get us out of that.

That means that we have to begin to put things into practice and stop just going through the motions. Do you

189

hear what I am saying? Here is what I need you to do. Today I want you to practice. I want you to practice hearing and listening.

Whatever comes to your mind, I want you to write it down. Take a pencil. Take a piece of paper, a pen, whatever it is you use — not a computer. Don't get to a computer and try to do this because that computer has too many other voices. *Facebook* is calling, *Twitter*, your emails. It is calling you. You can't do this on a computer. You need to get into a quiet place.

Get yourself something to write with; something to write on, and say:

> "Father, I am getting in this place. I want to
> hear Your voice. Speak to me."

You need to close your eyes. Just write down your thoughts. Write them down and then read them. And you will find that even in your thoughts — and some of you, it may be very clear that this is not just my thoughts. It is Father speaking to me.

He may speak to you audibly. He may give you an idea. He may even give you thoughts in your mind. But whatever it is, write it down. How many of you are willing to do that today? Don't just say it now. You have to do it. And you will be surprised. He may just, well, if He hasn't spoken to you in a while, today could be the day that He communicates. ∎

Shalom!

You have just enjoyed one of the many fine teac
through Arthur Bailey Ministries. Our full select
are available at:

www.ArthurBaileyMinistries.com

Are you interested in learning more about the *True Gospel* and how to better communicate the word of YeHoVaH? Here at Arthur Bailey Ministries, we now offer the world's first Messianic, Hebrew Roots of the Faith, **Discipleship Training Program.** This exclusive learning opportunity is available in workbook and DVD formats and also online here for individual or classroom study:

http://discipleship101.tv

Thank you for your interest in our products and ministry teachings! We invite you to participate in our fellowship services at House Of Israel in Charlotte; through one of our satellite locations, or via the Internet. Please see our web site for our weekly television broadcast schedule and live internet events. We are reaching, preaching, and teaching the *True Gospel of the Kingdom of YeHoVaH to the Whole World.* **We would be honored if you would join us!**

Fellowship Location		**Mailing Address**
House Of Israel		Arthur Bailey Ministries
1334 Hill Road		PO Box 49744
Charlotte, NC 28210		Charlotte, NC 28277

Office Phone | **Join us each week for our LIVE broadcasts**
888-899-1479 | Thursdays @ 7pm ET • Saturdays @ 11am ET

Taking the True Gospel of the Kingdom of YeHoVaH to the Whole World.

DVD Teachings By Arthur Bailey

In this 4-DVD teaching, Arthur Bailey expounds on each blessing; summarizes the 28 Blessings of *Deuteronomy 28,* and identifies what these blessings look like in our day and time. You will learn how these blessings manifest, and the importance of living a Torah Observant Spirit-Filled Life in order to experience the fullness of the "The 28 Blessings of Deuteronomy 28."

Approximately 5 hrs.

28 Blessings of Deuteronomy 28   4 DVDs – $45.00

In this exciting teaching you will learn what are considered to be the Firstfruits Offerings; when they are to be presented, and why Firstfruits Offerings are so important! You will also learn the prayer that is recited during this vital offering which assures the blessing of prosperity upon those who present this offering unto YeHoVaH.

Approximately 1.5 hrs.

Feast of Firstfruits
1 DVD – $15.00

DVD Teachings By Arthur Bailey

"Hear, O Israel" is a call for ALL of the People Of YeHoVaH to Hear and to Obey His Commands. Often times when people hear the word "Israel," they think "Jews." Israel consists of 12 Tribes; the Jews are only one of those tribes. In this eye-opening, engaging and life-changing teaching "Hear, O Israel," Arthur Bailey explains in-depth of Yeshua's response and the benefits of what it really means to Hear and to Obey! Approximately 2.5 hrs.

Hear, O Israel   2 DVDs – $25.00

In this dynamic, life-changing teaching: "How To Hear God's Voice," author and teacher Arthur Bailey shares important Biblical truths that will help you identify and distinguish the voice of the Almighty from all other voices. In this 4-DVD collection you will learn:

- Why YeHoVaH communicates with His people
- Why he wants you to hear His voice
- How to identify His voice from others
- Where he most likely speaks to you

And so much more! Approximately 5.5 hrs.

How To Hear God's Voice   4 DVDs – $45.00

DVD Teachings By Arthur Bailey

In this 2-DVD teaching series, Arthur Bailey presents from Scripture how the relationships in our lives must be categorized and prioritized according to their importance. You will learn:

- The kind of relationship the Almighty wants with you
- How to categorize and prioritize your relationships according to Scripture
- How to identify and rectify wrong relationships

And so much more! Approximately 2.5 hrs.

Relationships   2 DVDs – $25.00

Join Arthur Bailey as he explains the parable taught by Yeshua after having shared with His disciples about the Gospel of The Kingdom being preached to the whole world before the end comes. Yeshua gives a parable about three servants who were given specific talents. What distinguished the wise servant from the wicked servant in this parable was determined by what they did with the talents they had been given. Approximately 1.5 hrs.

Maximizing Your Talents   1 DVD – $15.00

DVD Teachings By Arthur Bailey

Where did Christmas originate? What does the Bible have to say about Christmas and its relationship to the birth of Christ? Is Christmas even in the Bible? Should Christ be in Christmas? Is Jesus the reason for the season? How should true believers respond to Christmas? These questions and so many more will be answered in this timeless Christmas Message, "MERRY CHRISTMAS?"
Approx. 1.5 hrs.

Merry Christmas?   1 DVD – $15.00

The ReNEWed Covenant is 1.5 hours of teaching. In this teaching "The ReNEWed Covenant," Arthur Bailey gives a clear, eye-opening, biblical explanation of what the New Covenant is, and with whom it is made. He explains how Jews and Gentiles enter into this covenant, and what it means for believers today. You will understand why it is called The ReNEWed Covenant, and the significant power that is released within the lives of all who embrace the ReNEWed Covenant. This Teaching Will Change Your Life Forever! Approximately 1.5 hrs.

The ReNEWed Covenant   1 DVD – $15.00

DVD Teachings By Arthur Bailey

In this powerful 4-DVD teaching "The Power of The Holy Spirit," author and teacher Arthur Bailey reveals the pre-requisites all believers must meet to be filled with the Holy Spirit and Power. What is this power Yeshua spoke of? Is this power still available for the disciples of Yeshua today? How can the disciples of Yeshua operate in this power today? These and many other questions will be answered in this fascinating and informative teaching series. Approximately 5.5 hrs.

The Power of the Holy Spirit   4 DVDs – $45.00

In this teaching Arthur Bailey will address:

- What is Prosperity?
- Is Prosperity Biblical?
- Is Poverty a Curse?
- Can Believers be Prosperous?
- What does the Bible Teach about Prosperity?
- What is True Biblical Prosperity?

What you believe about prosperity will determine what you can and cannot receive from YeHoVaH. This teaching series will leave you with a wealth of information. It will help you understand why YeHoVaH wants His people to be *prosperous*, and what *true Biblical prosperity* looks like! Approximately 5.5 hrs.

True Biblical Prosperity   4 DVDs – $45.00

DVD Teachings By Arthur Bailey

The Church world has taken a conversation Yeshua had with a Pharisee at night, and built powerhouse ministries teaching a gospel message of salvation and altar calls. Many sermons have been taught about being born again and what it should mean to believers today. But what does *John 3:16* really teach us within the context it is written? Like many other Biblical passages, this much-quoted verse is taught and preached in a manner that has become isolated from the passage context in which it was originally written. Approximately 2.5 hrs.

You Must Be Born Again   2 DVDs – $25.00

Paul wrote in the book of Romans, *"But God commendeth his love toward us, in that, while we were yet sinners, Messiah died for us"*. God demonstrated His love for us by giving His only begotten Son to die for our sins. How can we show our love for God? In this 4-DVD teaching, Arthur Bailey will take you on a journey through the *greatest love story ever written*, and what our response to the love of God

should be. It is more than just a story of salvation. It is a story of love; of overcoming, of victory, and of power. Approx. 5.5 hrs.

The Love of God   4 DVDs – $45.00

DVD Teachings By Arthur Bailey

The Fall Feasts of YeHoVaH is a 6-DVD set with over 6.5 hours of teaching. This series include teachings on The Feast of Trumpets/Yom Teruah, Day of Atonement/Yom Kippur, The Feast of Tabernacles/Sukkot and The Last Great Day/Shemini Atzeret. The Introduction to the Fall Feasts will not only provide insight and understanding of the prophetic shadow pictures of good things to come; it will also help us understand how to celebrate these amazing days in a way that pleases Almighty YeHoVaH.

The Fall Feasts Of YeHoVaH   6 DVDs – $65.00

Now Concerning Spiritual Gifts is a 6-DVD set with over 6.5 hours of teaching. Many suggest that the gifts of the Spirit have ceased to be in operation, just as they also insist that the Law is done away with. Among those who accept and teach that the spiritual gifts of the Bible are still operational today, many have abused and misused these gifts in their assembly; similar to those in the days of the Corinthian assembly Paul wrote to correct — thus the controversy! In this series,

Arthur Bailey takes the mystery out of manifesting spiritual gifts and empowers believers.

Now Concerning Spiritual Gifts   6 DVDs – $65.00

DVD Teachings By Arthur Bailey

The New Covenant — When did the New Covenant begin? Join Arthur Bailey as he journeys inside the first Jerusalem Council as the Apostles, Elders and Ruach Ha Kodesh discuss how to deal with a false teaching that was circulating among believers. Arthur Bailey is a spirit-filled, New Covenant minister who boldly teaches the Hebrew Roots of the Christian faith and takes the confusion out of covenants that are as important today as they were long ago. Includes two episodes.

The New Covenant   1 DVD – $15.00

Keeping Torah Living Spirit Filled. Join Arthur Bailey as he journeys inside the first Jerusalem Council as the Apostles,

Elders and Ruach Ha Kodesh discuss how to deal with a false teaching that was circulating among the believers and how to incorporate the Gentile converts into the newly formed Messianic community. This teaching will deepen your understanding of the early Hebrew culture and strengthen your walk in Yeshua Messiah. Three episodes. About 1.5 hours of teaching.

Keeping Torah Living Spirit Filled   1 DVD – $15.00

DVD Teachings By Arthur Bailey

The Baptism of the Holy Spirit — Yeshua said in Acts 1 verse 5: *"For John truly baptized with water; but ye shall be baptized with the Holy Ghost not many days hence."* And in verse 8: *"But ye shall receive power, after that the Holy Ghost is come upon you: and ye shall be witnesses unto me both in Jerusalem, and in all Judea, and in Samaria, and unto the uttermost parts of the earth."*

When we are baptized with the Holy Spirit, we receive power and authority not just to speak for YeHoVaH, but to demonstrate His power! In this 4-DVD teaching series, you will learn what is the true evidence of the baptism of the Holy Spirit and so much more! A must-have for every true believer who wants to walk in their authority. Over 5 hours of teaching!

The Baptism of the Holy Spirit   4 DVDs – $45.00

Walking in the Power of the Holy Spirit; My Testimony.   Join Arthur Bailey as he shares experiences and unique insights in this perceptive, sometimes hilarious and always instructive journey through his ministry spanning more than three decades. He generously shares his life-changing adventures of discovering and tapping back into the roots of the faith that he has long preached with boldness. As a former pastor and teacher in five different Christian denominations before coming to the true faith of the Kingdom of YeHoVaH, his unique story is priceless and required listening for those who desire to enhance their own walk in Torah-obedience and in Yeshua Messiah. About 1.5 hours of teaching.

Walking in the Power of the Holy Spirit; My Testimony
1 DVD – $20.00

And The Heavens Were Opened. In this 3 DVD series, Arthur Bailey takes you on an in-depth, inspiring journey through Shavuot, Yom Teruah and Hanukkah to reveal the importance of these biblical events for today's Spirit-filled believer in Yeshua. Learn more about operating in the gifts of the Holy Spirit, the works of Yeshua Messiah and the re-dedication of the second temple at Hanukkah. About 4.5 hours of teaching.

And The Heavens Were Opened   3 DVDs – $35.00

And You Shall Love The Lord... The Creator of the Universe demonstrated His love for us by sacrificing His only begotten Son for the sins of man. The Love of God is a gift! You can-not earn it. You do not deserve it. You cannot buy it. So how do we demon-strate our love for God? Often when sharing the Gospel of Yeshua (the Gospel Yeshua taught *not* the Gospel about Jesus), the subject of the "Law" comes up. Yeshua clearly stated that he did not come to do away with or to abolish the Law (Matthew 5:17). Yet people still argue that we must only "love" YeHoVaH with all of our heart, mind, soul and strength. Are we doing that? What does loving God look like? The Bible instructs us how YeHoVaH wants us to show our love for Him. Learn the truth and find answers to many questions you won't learn from religion. About 2.5 hours of teaching.

And You Shall Love The Lord...   2 DVDs – $25.00

DVD Teachings By Arthur Bailey

In this 2 DVD set, learn about how according to Acts 15, a major challenge existed which con-fronted the newly formed Messianic community. Arthur Bailey journeys in-side the first Jeru-salem Council where the Apostles, Elders and the Ruach Ha Kodesh discussed how to deal with a false teaching that was circulating among the early believers and how to incorporate Gentile converts into the newly formed Messianic community. Many traditional Jewish believers in Yeshua struggled with how to go from a totally ethnic Jewish religious community to one which included non-Hebrew people who were unfamiliar with the rich heritage and traditions formed by the Pharisees and handed down by the Elders. This teaching will deepen and strengthen your spiritual walk in Yeshua Messiah as you learn more about the history of the early called-out ones of faith. 2 episodes.

What Do We Do With Those Gentiles?   1 DVD – $15.00

Today there is as much confusion about being "Messianic" as there is on certain issues across denominational Christianity. As more and more people's eyes are opened to the faith once delivered to the saints and new believers are being added to the family of YeHoVaH, it is vitally important that they get started on the path the right way. In this very important  teaching, Arthur Bailey shares what every new believer must know to live a power-filled, successful life in the Kingdom of YeHoVaH. You will learn who you are in Messiah, the importance of the faith, the baptism of the Holy Spirit, how to properly respond to the Sabbath argument, the dietary laws and feast days and much more. About 2 hours of teaching.

Messianic 101: "The Essentials"   2 DVDs – $25.00

The DVDs listed in this book are just a sampling of the many teaching DVDs produced by Arthur Bailey Ministries. These teaching DVDs are packed with scriptural references and are taught in a format that will encourage, strengthen, and enhance your spiritual journey to help you grow to maturity in Messiah Yeshua.

Please be certain to enroll in our Discipleship Training Program. It is the only Messianic Hebrew Roots of the faith program on the planet! Learn more about the true history of the faith once delivered to the saints and prepare yourself for ministry services and/or ordination. This is a comprehensive program that is at a collegiate level for all true believers today, no matter where they are in their walk. This series of 105 classes can be viewed online. There are also workbooks available for purchase and that are designed to accompany this two-year Discipleship course. Visit the Discipleship Training Program's web site:

http://discipleship101.tv

Stop in at our ministry web site to order any of the DVDs, books and other teaching materials and supplies available through our online store.

www.ArthurBaileyMinistries.com/Bookstore

In addition to placing your order online on our secure website, you may also call in your orders at 1-888-899-1479, or send your check or money order to:

Arthur Bailey Ministries
P.O. Box 49744
Charlotte, NC 28277

Your Support is Highly Appreciated.

Be Blessed in Yeshua Messiah! Shalom!

Made in the USA
San Bernardino, CA
17 April 2015